The Tree of Light
The Lives of the Prophets for Young Muslims
Volume 1

adaptation by
Elizabeth Bootman

This book is dedicated to my sons.
May Allah (s) bless all our children and help us to teach them
about the example of the Prophets (a).

ISBN: 9781980454076

TABLE OF CONTENTS

Introduction

This work is an adaptation of the Lore of Light by Hajjah Amina Adil. Her comprehensive and beautiful recounting of the lives of the Prophets is the primary resource for this history. If you would like to know more about the lives of the Prophets please see her full work, Lore of Light, and if you would like to read an elementary level version of these stories please see My Little Lore of Light adapted by Karima Sperling.

In this history, the stories are told by a sage who happens to be the grandfather of two adventurous boys who are hoping to one day attend a famous school of Sufi teaching called Al Chemya. This part of the book is a fictional framing story to help make these histories interesting and relevant to young adult readers.

Most of the artwork are hand painted watercolors styled after Persian miniatures and archaeological sites and maqams of the Prophets and their families. Please see our website for more project ideas to help young Muslims learn about the lives of the Prophets at:

https://muslimfamilytraditions.wordpress.com

"And we have honored the children of Adam."

Sulayman and Yusuf were playing in the garden of their Grandfather. Sulayman climbed the branches of the apple tree and dropped an apple on Yusuf's head and kept climbing as Yusuf cried and scuttled after his big brother. Yusuf slid down the trunk unable to reach the lowest branch and sank to the ground next to the apple.

Their Grandfather found Yusuf and helped him up, cleaned the apple for him and rubbed his sore head before shooting a reproving look at his naughty brother above. Sulayman hid behind a branch feeling ashamed and wanting to disappear.

Grandfather sat under the tree with Yusuf and told him to eat his apple. "Do you know the story of the Tree of Knowledge and our Father Adam (a)?" Grandfather asked.

Yusuf shook his head, juice running down his chin, eyes wide with interest. Grandfather took a handkerchief from his pocket and wiped Yusuf's face gently. "Then I will tell you his story, and when I am done you can tell me if you think your brother should be punished." Grandfather glanced upward and Sulayman hid again making the tree sway.

1 ADAM (a)

Once upon a time in a garden far far away there was a man named Adam (a) that was created by his Lord from clay, water and divine breath.

When Allah (s) wished to create Adam (a) He sent his angels to the earth to bring Him clay. Angels brought clay from all the corners of the earth and from heaven and from hell and from the core of the earth. Allah (s) took this clay and formed it into the shape of a man, but this was only a shape, a physicality, until Allah (s) added one more and most important ingredient.

"Do you know what it was?" asked Grandfather.

A butterfly landed on Grandfather's walking stick and Yusuf giggled and pointed at it.

"When Allah (s) wished to bring his creation to life he gave breath to Adam (a), and he came to life with the light of Muhammad (s)."

Grandfather gently blew on the butterfly and it fluttered and flew away.

A great master named Mevlana Jalaluddin Rumi once said that the creation is unfolding here on earth something like this:

I died as a mineral and became a plant.
I died as a plant and rose to an animal,
I died as an animal and I was a Man.
Why should I fear?
When was I less by dying?

Yet once more I shall die as a Man, to soar with blessed angels, but even from this I must pass on because all except Allah will perish.

When I have sacrificed this soul, I shall become what no mind before conceived. Oh, please let me pass into nothingness, please let me to be annihilated and return to The One who made me.

"How is Allah making us from clay? Where is my clay?" asked Sulayman, sliding down to a lower branch looking at his hand.

"Hmm," smiled Grandfather. "Many people are interested in how, but the people who understand more ask why Sulayman. And for real understanding you must know both. I am saying that the unfolding of creation is more than we can understand. If creation is like a large banquet table, then we are seeing the creation of Allah (s) like our dinner at that table. The food is arriving at the table one dish after another. Some are saying that the food arrives, cooked, seasoned, heated and chilled perfectly by accident. They say there is no chef, there is only an oven and pots and pans cooking but no recipe; there is no waiter to bring the food. They are thinking that the food cooks itself randomly alone in the kitchen." Grandfather chuckled.

Yusuf pointed up above his head, "I see table now."

"Then there are others, who eat the food at the other end of the table. They are no mind ones as well. They say that the food has no oven has no need of cooking, no recipe no work to make it and takes no time to prepare. They say Allah (s) is making like this with magic wand 'puff.' They have faith but no mind. I am liking to sit in the middle and I am laughing at them both because if you are knowing the truth many things are very funny. There is a chef, there is an oven, there are ingredients, and the chef has a recipe for his creation. Each recipe has its time to prepare and to cook and then Lord of Heavens is sending his creation to earth with angels who are like the waiters. Do not believe the people who are thinking there is no chef and do not believe the people who think there is no kitchen for they are both having no mind, but they are very funny." Grandfather took his prayer beads from his pocket and began his recitation.

Then Allah (s) created the ego. Many trials were given to the disobedient ego but it only became more defiant, more naughty.

"Do I have an ego?" asked Sulayman. "I make everyone cross when I am naughty."

Grandfather started laughing and rubbed Sulayman's head as tears ran down his cheeks.

Then the Lord placed the ego in the Valley of Hunger, and after it stayed there for a long time the ego recognized Allah (s) as its Lord. This is why we are not eating in Ramadan. We are training our egos to be obedient and not wild crazy ones.

The angels bowing to Adam (a) on the order of their Lord.

The soul entered this clay form and the heart began to beat with the dhikr of Allah (s). Adam (a) was taught the names of all the things in creation. Within Adam (a) was placed a special light, and the angels bowed low to Adam (a), but Iblis did not obey because he could not see this light; he was only seeing the clay.

> *"Where were all the other people?" asked Sulayman. "Where was Adam's family?"*

> *"Hmm." Grandfather looked up. "If Allah blesses us with family then we have to be kind and gentle with them or we will be alone and unhappy."*

Adam (a) was lonely in the garden and Allah (s) created Hawa (r) so that they would be together. They were asked to not eat the fruit of one tree there in the garden. They were deceived by Iblis who entered the garden inside the peacock.

He deceived Adam (a) and Hawa (r) with fear and lies, telling
them that they would suffer a terrible death if they did not eat the
fruit of the forbidden wheat tree. They regretted their error and
dressed themselves with the leaves of the fig tree because they
were ashamed. Some are saying they were ashamed because
they were naked but when we do wrong sometimes we are hiding,
wanting to hide what we have done and hide ourselves from
punishment.

*Grandfather glanced up into the tree where Sulayman
was hiding. Sulayman hid behind the branch again.*

"Do not forget that we cannot hide from the things that we have done and do not forget that it is written that we have done these things so that we can learn from our mistakes and ask for forgiveness." Grandfather rubbed Yusuf's head again and took his miswak tooth stick from his pocket.

Adam (a) descended to earth and landed on Mt. Serendib in Sri Lanka and Hawa (r) landed in Jeddah in Saudi Arabia.

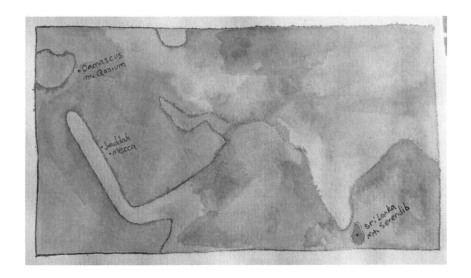

Adam (a) and Hawa (r) sought forgiveness and it was granted to them. Adam (a) and Hawa (r) were reunited at Arafat after they had completed the Hajj. Adam (a) was asked to build the Kaaba. Then they began to farm the land with oxen and grain from Angel Jibrail (a). Adam (a) was given a staff from heaven that would later be given to Musa (a) and a ring that would later be given to Sulayman (a).

Grandfather took off his ring and handed it to Yusuf who was fidgeting now that his apple was finished.

Hawa (r) had many children and among them were Qabil and Habil. Habil was a shepherd with flocks of sheep and Qabil was a farmer. Each of them offered sacrifices, like a gift, to their Lord, but only Habil's was accepted. This and other jealousies between them caused enmity and Qabil killed his brother with a rock on Mt. Qasiyun in Damascus in the Cavern of Blood.

We must always remember that jealousy and bad feelings will harm us and the people we love. Qabil regretted what he did to Habil but he could not take it back. We must not be heedless ones. We must use our mind and think before we do an action, this is why Allah (s) gave us a mind.

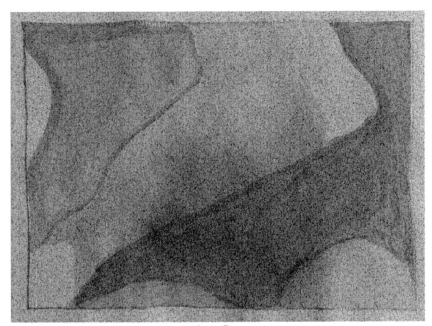

The Cave

After a life of 1,000 years Adam (a) passed away and was buried
on Mt. Serendib where he fell to earth and left Paradise. In our
time, we are blessed to only spend around 100 years or so away
from our creator.

Mt. Serendib

Sulayman climbed down from the tree and kissed his brother, apologizing for the apple. Yusuf hugged his brother and tried to climb the tree again. "Up up in the tree." he said. They climbed the tree together while Grandfather took a nap.

Grandfather found Sulayman and Yusuf in their room with their heads in the toy chest and their bottoms hanging out trying to reach all their stray blocks. They built a little city with the blocks and were just a few pieces shy. They did not want to come to dinner till it was finished. Grandfather waited patiently as they placed the last pieces. Then he promised to tell them a story about a very beautiful and important chest after they had eaten their dinner and helped their mother wash up.

2 SETH (a)

When Adam (a) and Hawa (r) had lost their son Habil they were heartbroken, but Allah (s) sent them another son in his place to strengthen them. His name was Seth (a) and he was a prophet that received 50 pages of Allah's (s) words of guidance to human kind.

"Where is his book?" Sulayman asked.

"Allah (s) knows, it may be near or far," Grandfather answered.

"What was his book about?" Sulayman asked.

"That is not known, but Allah (s) taught Seth's (a) father Adam (a) the names of all things. Maybe this book was about the names of things, or maybe it is like the Psalms of Dawud (a), stories like the Injil or like the Quran."

"Where are all the books now?"

"Allah (s) has given them to the Saints for safe keeping."

"Can I read them, I am learning to read."

"Some books of Allah (s) are written in very old languages, languages that are not spoken anymore."

"So, I can't read them?"

"If Allah (s) wants you to know what is in these books maybe you could."

Sulayman frowned. "But I want to see them. I want to try to read them."

"That is a good intention. You should ask Allah (s) for this, make a dua prayer every day. Maybe it will open for you."

This prophecy was kept in a beautiful chest called the ark that we will learn more about when we hear the story of Prophet Musa (a).

"Why will we learn more about the ark when we hear the story of Musa?"

"In the story of Musa (a) the ark receives more books from Allah (s)."

"What books?"

"The Tawrat."

"What is that?"

"It is the Holy Book given to Musa (a) for the Banu Israil."

"Can I see that too?"

"Yes. That book is known."

Grandfather went to his bookshelf. He took down several books and laid them on the table before Sulayman.

"This is the Tawrat, this is the Bible and this is the Quran. Some of the Psalms of Dawud (a) are in the bible."

Sulayman picked them up one by one and looked through each hand painted page with colors and gold leaf.

"Mama says I can't touch your books or your bookshelf."

"They are old books," Grandfather nodded.

"Did Allah (s) really write them?"

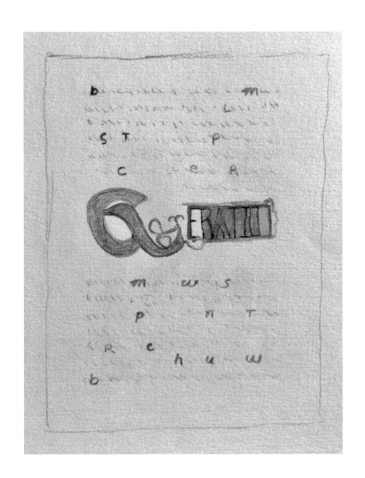

23

"Allah (s) wrote the originals. Some of these have been changed a bit but they still contain wisdom."

Grandfather put the books back on the shelf.

"So, all the books are in the ark? Are they there now?"

Grandfather smiled. "Yes, yes they are."

"Where is the ark? Can I see it?"

"It is not far. And one day if Allah (s) gives permission you may see it. Maybe you have already seen it and did not know what it was."

Sulayman frowned. "I want to read all of Allah's (s) books."

"Why?"

"Well if I read all of Allah's books then I will know everything that Allah (s) said."

Grandfather laughed, "If all the trees were pens and all the oceans were ink the words of Allah (s) could not be exhausted. Not everything that Allah (s) said is written in a book here on earth."

"That's a lot of books," Sulayman looked doubtful. "Is that what the angels do? Do they read all of Allah's ocean books?"

Grandfather smiled. "Maybe."

The prophets who receive the books of Allah (s) are called messengers and they have a special responsibility to teach us about these books, help us to understand the books and show us how to follow the books.

"Allah gave all the prophets a book?"

"No, not to all."

"Why not? I thought Allah has oceans of books."

Grandfather smiled. "I think one day Sulayman that you are going to be a very great scholar."

"What is a scholar?"

"Hmm. Scholars are having many many questions. But their sadness is that they are not having many answers to their many many questions."

"You answer my questions Grandfather."

Grandfather laughed. "One day Allah (s) will call for me and who will you ask then?"

Sulayman frowned. "But I don't know anyone as smart as you. When I ask anything, everyone tells me I must ask you. Who taught you Grandfather? Who did you ask all your questions to?"

"I asked many questions when I was young. I spoke to many people of knowledge and read many books but real teaching, real knowledge is with my Master."

"Where is he?"

"He is in the grave."

"How do you ask him then?"

"I still speak to my Master."

"How?"

"Like this." Grandfather took his tasbih prayer beads out of his pocket and held them up to his ear saying "Allo, allo," like a telephone.

Sulayman frowned. "You are making fun of me."

Yusuf put his ear to the beads and said "Allo, allo." He looked up at Grandfather. "He hanged up," Yusuf shrugged.

Seth (a) was the first prophet to bring a book from Allah (s) and Prophet Muhammad (s) was The Last Prophet to bring a book from Allah (s).

In the beginning the people had lived underground, but that had changed and in this time, there were two groups of people. The people who lived in the mountains and followed the prophecies of Adam (a) and Seth (a) and the people who lived in the valleys and cities near the water that followed the wicked ways of Qabil who slew his brother and did not follow the word of Allah (s).

Mevlana Rumi (q) tells the story of Seth (a).

These misguided people wanted to kill Adam (a) and worshipped idols instead of Allah (s). They remembered that human kind came from paradise and blamed Adam (a) for their fall. At this time Allah (s) made human kind to have many different languages so that these misguided people could not succeed in their evil plan to kill their father Adam (a).

"Is that why the books of Allah are in different languages?"

"Hmm. The books of Allah (s) are in the same family of languages. Over time languages change but yes in a way the books I showed you are in different languages because the language of people changes. The heavenly language stays the same."

The grave of Seth (a) is said to be in the Kingdom of Jordan and Allah (s) knows best.

The Maqam where people honour Seth (a) in Lebanon.

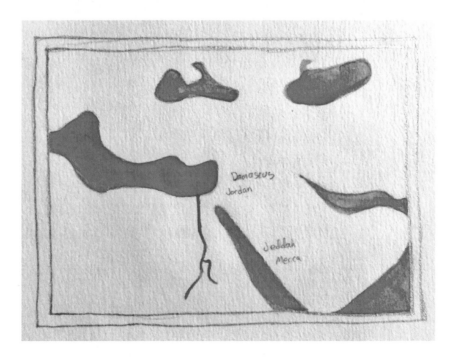

Grandfather looked down at the boys and saw that they were asleep. As he rose to go his toe hit another toy block. He picked it up and opened the chest carved with beautiful long faded wings all along the sides. He looked inside at the stacks of wound up velum and large carved stones and chuckled, "Come now, not that ark, bring the toys back," he tapped the box with his stick, telling it to behave. He closed the lid once more and whispered a special prayer, "Authu bi kalimat-illah hil-tammah min sharri ma kahlaqa"[1] opening it again to see a pile of wood blocks. He placed the last block and closed the lid, saying "Keela mea makkannee feehi raabee haayrun fa aeenoonee bi kuvvatin ac'aal baynakum va baynahumm radman,"[2] before turning out the light as the athan (call to prayer) began and stars twinkled in the sky above the courtyard.

---

[1] "I seek refuge in the perfect words of Allah from the evil that which He has created."

[2] "That in which my Lord has strengthened me is better. Only my Lord will help me with that Force. I will make a shield force between you and them." (Al Kaf 95)

"For man is more than the sum of his parts." Aristotle

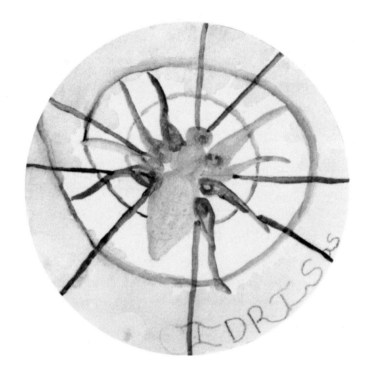

3 IDRIS (a)

Sulayman and Yusuf were having their Quran lesson.
Sulayman sat with his lawh wood board and ink writing the
ayat.

Yusuf tipped over his ink and stained his clothes and the carpet. Sulayman jumped up trying to escape the flood. Yusuf started crying and Grandfather came to see what was wrong. He took Yusuf to change his clothes and patted his head when he returned to the lesson.

"I don't want to write Quran anymore Grandfather. I want to go play," whined Sulayman.

"Hmm," said Grandfather, taking Sulayman's lawh. He looked down at the lawh and the ayat written there.

"If you finish your lesson and memorize this ayat I will tell you the story of the one who brought writing, and clothes, and many other things to human beings."

Sulayman thought about it for a minute. Yusuf started reciting the ayat. Yusuf could not write yet really but he was learning to recite. Sulayman scowled because Yusuf had already memorized the lesson. He did not want his brother to exceed him so he sat down and began practicing.

After lunch, it was time for Yusuf to have a nap and Grandfather usually took him to rest. Sulayman followed because Grandfather said it was time to hear the story.

"But I am not taking a nap Grandfather," said Sulayman. "I am too big for naps."

"Hmm," said Grandfather. "I am not too big for naps."

They settled down on the cushions to get cozy.

"Who is the one who made the writing? I don't like him because I don't like to write," said Sulayman.

"Hmm," Grandfather chuckled. "The people of Idris (a) did not like him very much either at one time. But then they realized that he brought so many good things to make their lives better that they finally loved him and followed him."

"What things?" said Yusuf. Grandfather rubbed his head and began his tale.

The Prophet Idris (a) was a shepherd like the prophets before him, but then he became an inventor. He learned to make fire, build houses, write words and read them.

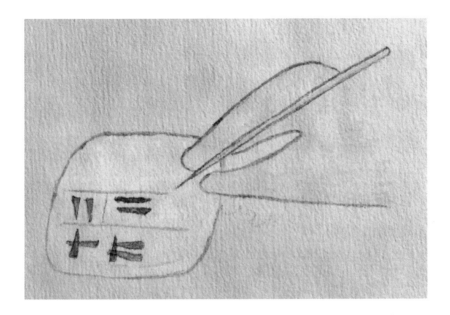

Idris (a) learned to do sums, and to read the stars and to find his direction. He became a teacher for his people and wrote the books of Adam (a) and Seth(a). Before this time people would memorize stories but they could not write them down. Today we write the Quran but we still memorize it so that even if all the books in the world were lost the Quran would not be lost.

"Does that mean I don't have to write Quran if I memorize it."

"You can memorize without writing, but writing helps us to memorize as well. Writing has many uses though. One day you will see how important writing is for your life."

Idris (a) knew the lore of healing plants and became the first doctor to his people. At that time people thought that ill health came from magic but Idris (a) taught his people that Allah (s) sends illness so that we might seek our cure from the remedies sent by our Lord. He also taught his people to dry and store food for the winter.

"What did they do if someone got sick?" asked Sulayman.

"Hmm, sometimes they thought that there was a witch or a sorcerer doing magic on them or something like this. They would look for the one who made them sick. This is very bad because even today no mind people look for the one who made them sick instead of asking their Lord for help and looking for their remedy. When people believe like this they hurt many innocent people and they cannot cure themselves. We are very fortunate ones that learned the truth from Idris (a).

At this time, human beings did not wear clothes as we wear today. They wore smelly animal skins because they had nothing else to wear. One day Idris (a) saw a spider weaving its web and said that Allah (s) had taught him to make cloth. He understood that Allah (s) was teaching him all the time and he should listen to the lessons.

Grandfather looked sideways at Sulayman who was fidgeting and annoying his brother.

Idris (a) had learned to spin yarn from his grandmother Eve and he took that yarn and wove cloth on a loom that he made. He had been blessed with a clever wife – Hadama. She liked his invention and helped him to make the cloth. When the cloth was ready they prayed to Allah (s) to show them what to do with it. When that inspiration came Idris (a) asked Hadama to lie down on the cloth as a pattern that he drew in coal. Idris (a) used stones to cut the cloth and thorns to sew it. Idris (a) found his wife to be very beautiful in this gown and Idris became the first tailor. Hadama made a gown for Idris and they shared their invention with the people and taught them about the uses of cloth.

"What did they do with the animal skins?" asked Sulayman.

"I have shirt!" squeaked Yusuf trying to show Grandfather his clean shirt.

Grandfather looked down at the boys and yawned.
"They used the animal skins to make shoes and boots and other useful things."

We are called by our Lord to strive beyond the circumstances of our birth and to reach higher in ability and understanding, but the people of this time were of low understanding and feared the knowledge and innovation that Idris (a) brought. The people were like the no mind people you find today saying "shirk!" and "biddah!" Some people cannot see the difference between something that is a good invention and something that is bad for them. At first, they were afraid of all these new inventions and wanted Idris (a) to go away. When they thought about it though they realized that all the things that Idris (a) brought them had improved their lives and they decided to follow him. People then did not know many things but they could think. People now know many things but they cannot think.

"Is writing a good invention? It hurts me hand," said Sulayman.

"Hmm," Grandfather opened his eyes. "Writing some things is good. Writing Quran is good. You can write letters also. One day you will be very happy you learned. Now you are frustrated because today people want children to learn things before they understand how to use them. Tomorrow I will help you write a letter to your Baba. He will receive it before he returns from Hajj. Would you like that?"

"Will Baba write me a letter?" asked Sulayman.

"Yes. And you can ask him about all the things he is seeing there."

Yusuf started crying. "I want letter!" Grandfather patted his tummy.

"Yusuf can write a letter too. I will help you."

Idris (a) was warned that unbelievers were coming to destroy him and that he must defend himself. He was inspired to make a bow and arrows. He saw veins of metal in the stones of cooking fires and heated the stones to extract the metal to make swords and spears and then he taught the people to defend themselves. The sons of Cain had been preparing as well with their own instruments of war but they were easily defeated by the small army of believers.

"Can I have a bow and arrow," asked Sulayman.

Grandfather stared at Sulayman for a moment. "Bow and arrow are dangerous for boys who cannot write. The bow and arrow need much strength in the hands and if writing hurts you a bow and arrow will be too difficult."

Sulayman looked down at his hands. He scowled.

"Sulayman if you are keeping that face all the time it will get stuck that way and then even when you are happy you will look like you ate a lemon."

Sulayman looked scared and ran to look in the mirror.

Idris (a) was then inspired to tame and ride camels and later horses. Horses are far more delicate than camels and not as well adapted to a hot and dry climate, but they were very fast. Before Prophet Idris (a) people had to walk everywhere and carry everything, but now they had helpers.

"Can I have a camel Grandfather?" asked Sulayman "Mama said no but I rode one with Baba in the desert. It wasn't dangerous."

"Yusuf no like camel!" Yusuf hid under his blanket.

"Your mother doesn't think the camel was dangerous. She just doesn't have a place to put a camel."

"We can put the camel on the terrace and he can take me to school. But not Yusuf. He didn't like the camel. He was afraid because the camel was so high."

"Your mother has no place for a camel on the terrace." Grandfather started laughing and patting the lump that was Yusuf under the blanket.

Idris (a) retired to a cave to worship his Lord and angels came to visit him there. The angel of the sun came often to Idris (a), and on his last visit he brought him to visit the throne of the sun, where he passed away. The angel awoke him on the throne and told Idris (a) that he had died. Idris (a) asked to see Hell and so the angel took him to the Sirat bridge and he looked down into Hell below the bridge.

Then the angel took Idris (a) to Paradise. Idris (a) now dwells in Paradise and is the tailor of the people there.

Grandfather looked down at the boys. They were both snoring. Grandfather took off his turban and set it down, taking care not to disturb the angel that sat on the top of the cone, and lay down to rest a bit before the Asr prayer.

This is thought to be the place where Prophet Idris (a) prayed.

This is the maqam of the Prophet Idris (a) in Iraq.

Map of the Near East showing the regions concerning this story.

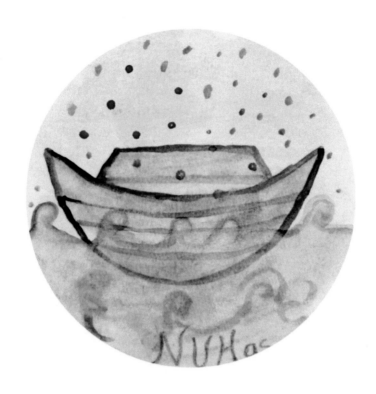

4 NUH (a)

*Sulayman and Yusuf were playing in the garden
fountain with little toy boats carved out of wood.
Sulayman took a huge bucket of water and threw it
on the boat that Yusuf was floating and suddenly
there was screaming and crying and splashing.
Grandfather came out of the orchard to see what
was wrong.*

There was water all over the tiles; both boys were soaked through and looked very unhappy. He looked into the fountain and saw the boat still bouncing along in the water. It had not sunk even with all the commotion. Grandfather had made the boys these matching boats as gifts for Ashura.

"Hmm," said grandfather. "Yusuf is this your boat?"

Yusuf nodded.

"Come Yusuf. We will get you some dry clothes and I will tell you the story of the most famous boat that was ever made." Yusuf took Grandfather's hand and they shuffled off together leaving Sulayman behind by the fountain.

Yusuf sat on the couch in warm fresh clothes wrapped in a blanket sucking his thumb. Sulayman sat across the room on the other couch swinging his legs back and forth impatiently.

Grandfather took out his prayer beads and put down his tea.

"The Prophet Nuh (a) was the son of Lamaq who saw terrible things in the caves near Babylon. There was a snake king called Zahaq that would kill and eat his people.

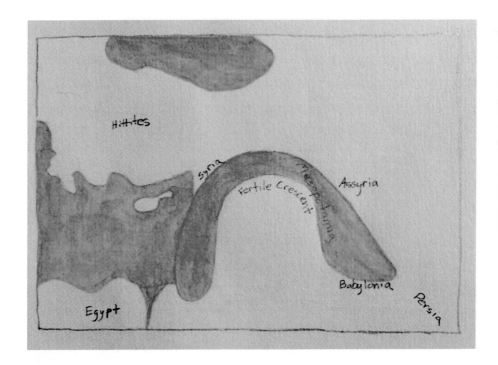

In this time Lamaq and Nuh (a) hid their religion from the people. The king Zahaq was cruel to the slaves of his nation and Nuh (a) was horrified by their plight. Nuh (a) worked as a carpenter for the king and made beautiful carvings for the palace for 10 years.

> *"Why did the snake king eat the people?" asked Sulayman.*

> *Yusuf took his thumb out of his mouth and hid it under the blanket.*

Grandfather looked at Yusuf and patted the blanket.
"King Zahaq was believing that he was God because he
listened to the counsel of Iblis (Shaitan). Those ones who
listen to Iblis are pushed to do very horrible things."
Grandfather pinched one of Yusuf's toes gently through
the blanket and Yusuf squealed and pulled the blanket
over his head.

Then Prophet Nuh (a) was called by the Angel Mikail (a), and for ten years he traveled with him and saw the condition of men around the world. After that Nuh (a) was called to prophethood by the Angel Jibrail (a). This was a very difficult task because the people had forgotten the difference between right and wrong and would not listen to Nuh (a).

Before the flood came to destroy the disbelievers, there had been a drought for 40 years. During this time, no children were born. The flood was coming and Nuh (a) knew this. The angel Jibrail (a) brought Nuh (a) the order for the ark to be built and the time was near. Nuh (a) employed the help of a giant named Uj to bring the wood. The giant was always very hungry and Nuh (a) said that he would feed him well.

"How big was the giant?" asked Sulayman.

Grandfather took an old book down from his shelf and turned the pages slowly before turning the book towards the boys.

The giant brought an arm full of trees as building wood. Nuh (a) convinced him to say "Bissmillah ar-Rahman ir Rahim"[1] before he began to eat the two loaves of bread. Soon the giant was feeling very full and took most of the wood with him in anger, because he thought he'd been tricked. Yet the small pieces of wood left behind were sufficient to build he ark.

"Why did the giant think he was tricked?" Sulayman asked.

"The giant did not understand why he was full."

---

[1] "In the name of God, the most gracious, the most merciful."

"Why did Bissmillah ar-Rahman ir Rahim make him feel full?"

"Hmm. When we begin an action with Bissmillah we are asking for Allah to make our action good and successful. If we want to be full from our food we will feel satisfied if we say Bissmillah."

"I want chocolate!" Yusuf squeaked.

"Me too!" said Sulayman.

Grandfather reached into his pocket and took out two chocolates. The boys said Bissmillah when they ate them and were very happy.

Jibrail (a) gave the instructions to build the ark. There were to be 124,000 planks and upon each plank would be written the name of a prophet. Four additional planks would carry the names of the four caliphs following the Prophet Muhammad (s) and two more for his grandsons Hassan and Hussain. These blessed names were the protection upon the ark from the Sea of Wrath that would descend onto earth and destroy the world.

"Why are there so many prophets grandfather?" asked Sulayman.

"Hmm." Grandfather paused for a moment. "The people that Allah (s) created have not been left on this earth without guidance. Every people on earth have received the wisdom of Allah (s) through their prophets."

While Nuh (a) was building the ark, the unbelievers threw dirty things all over the area. A skin disease was set upon the people as a divine punishment and its only cure was to clean the ulcers with the dirt they had thrown in the ark. So, the unbelievers had to come to the ark to be cured and so cleaned all the dirt away.

The front part of the ark was shaped like the breastbone of a bird and the back part of the boat was shaped like the tail of a peacock.

This is where some say the flood began in Iraq.

Nuh (a) knew that the sign of the flood being near would be that water would gush up from the bread ovens. The unbelievers did not see how that could be in a land with no rain.

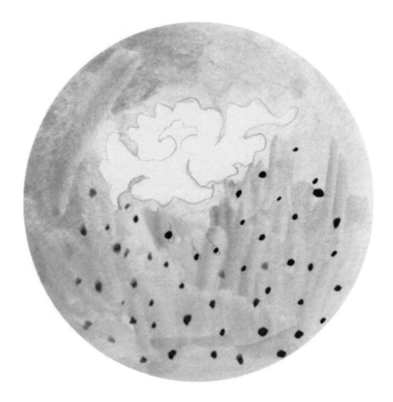

When the sign appeared the boarding of the ark began. The animals boarded the first tier of the boat. Iblis took hold of the donkey's tail to stop him and Nuh (a) urged the donkey to get in by calling him a "damned one." In this way Iblis was invited onto the ark as he is damned indeed.

The human beings boarded the second tier of the boat and the birds boarded the third tier. There were 80 believers and the family of Nuh (a) who boarded the ark. After the doors were closed water came from above and below.

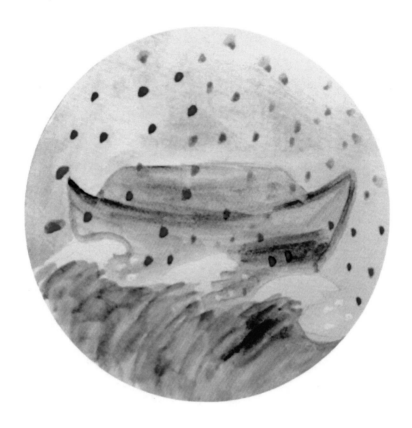

"Why did Allah (s) let Iblis get on the boat?"

"Hmmm." Grandfather smiled. "That is a very good question. Why do you think Allah (s) let Iblis sneak into the boat?"

Sulayman thought for a moment; it appeared to be painful to think so hard.

Grandfather chuckled. "Sulayman, when you are in a dark room with no light can you see where you are going?"

"No."

"If you are in the dark and come out in the sun where it is very bright can you see anything before your eyes adjust?"

"No."

"Everything that Allah (s) created has its purpose. The light and the dark make a shadow that allows us to see the shape of things. You must contemplate these things. It is the work of your life to understand them."

Nuh (a) had one son named Kenan who could not believe his father's prophecy and so did not follow him. The rain drops fell like millstones, the waves came like mountains, and the son of Nuh (a) was among the drowned.

When Iblis was discovered aboard the ark he told Nuh (a) that his nation would be destroyed by 5 things, 2 of which he named, greed and envy. Iblis said that he had been envious of Adam (a), and Adam (a) had been greedy to eat of the Tree of Knowledge in Eden.

There were 3 animals created on the ark. When Nuh (a) stroked the elephant, it sneezed and the pig was created. This pig consumed all the dirt on the boat so that it was kept clean. Iblis stroked the back of the pig and the rat was born. Nuh (a) stroked the back of the lion and the housecat was born to control the rats, but not before they had gnawed a hole in the hull of the ark. The snake stopped the hole with its tail and so saved the ark.

"Was it a rattlesnake?" asked Sulayman.

"I do not think so," replied Grandfather.

"Was it a cobra?" asked Sulayman.

Yusuf swayed from side to side like a cobra and Grandfather laughed.

When the rains had stopped Nuh (a) sent the crow to search for dry land, but the crow found a dead animal, or some say the son of Nuh (a), on a mountain and did not return. So Nuh (a) sent the dove. The dove found an olive tree, but its legs touched the Sea of Wrath while taking the olive twig and the feathers fell off and the legs turned red. Nuh (a) blessed the dove when it returned and cursed the crow.

After some time, the ark came to rest on Mount Judi on the Day of Ashura. Ashura is also the name for the sweet pudding they made from all the leftover food on the ark.

This is a photo of Ashura pudding that
is still made to celebrate the holiday.

After they had landed Nuh (a) found the earth to be white from
all the bones of the drowned creatures. Nuh (a) wept at the
vastness of this destruction. Allah (s) instructed Nuh (a) to take
clay and make earthenware vessels and pile them up high.

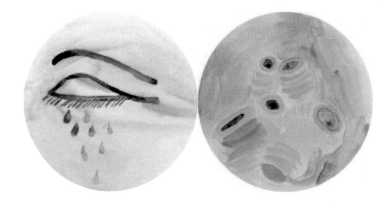

Then he was told to pull out the pot on the bottom, so causing all of them to fall and break. Nuh (a) was anguished by the destruction of all his hard work. In this way Allah (s) showed to Nuh (a) what it is like for a creator to destroy his own creation, as when Allah (s) accepted the prayer of Nuh (a) and destroyed the unbelievers and their world. Nuh (a) was warned not to pray against anyone ever again or his name would be erased from the book of prophets.

There was one widowed lady that was a believer and had asked Nuh (a) not to forget her when the time would come to board the ark, but he did forget. When the water had subsided, she came to Nuh (a) and he asked where she had been. She said she had been at home awaiting word to board the ark. One day, she told him, her cow came home with muddy feet and she was wondering why as there was no cloud in the sky that she could see. Allah (s) had protected the lady from the flood even though she did not board the ark.

Nuh (a) is known as the second father of mankind after Adam (a) because only his children had babies after the flood. The maqam of Nuh (a) is said to be at Kufa and the ark to be on Mount Qaf, but this is not for certain, and Allah (s) knows best.

There are two maqams that people visit to
honour Nuh (a). One in Cizre.

Another maqam of Prophet Nuh (a) is in Jordan.

Interior of the Maqam

Grandfather looked over at the boys as he finished his tale and they were sleeping. A white dove flew in from the courtyard and sat on Grandfather's shoulder. It whispered something in his ear and Grandfather responded. The dove cooed and flew away.

5 HOOD (a)

On a sunny day Grandfather took the boys to the botanical garden on the edge of the city. They ran up and down the arcades lined with palm trees and splashed each other with the water in the fountain while Grandfather walked after them with his prayer beads and walking stick. Sulayman took a bamboo branch and started to harass Yusuf with it until Grandfather made a play sword fight with him using his walking stick.

When they got tired the boys sat under an orange tree
while grandfather slowly peeled fruit for them. He took a
seed from the sweetest orange and put it in his pocket,
then he told them the story of the most famous garden that
was ever made on earth. It was called the Gardens of Iram.

When Prophet Nuh (a) reached the end of his life he returned
with his sons to Babylon, from where he then sent Sem to Arabia
and Yemen. Sem was told to settle near where the Kaaba had
been before the flood. After the flood, the people believed and
worshiped The One God of Nuh(a). Many hundred years later
they had forgotten and begun to worship idols again. These idols
appeared to speak but it was a trick. One tribe of Arabia called
Ad had a priest who convinced their king that he was a god by
saying he had seen this in a dream.

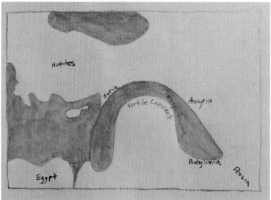

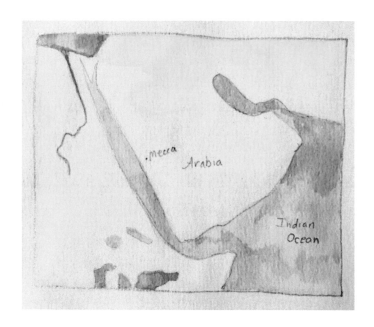

The king and the priest conspired to trick the people so that they believed that their king was also their god. They then brought the mob to the cave where other priests from their people had hidden and they killed them and ate them. There-after the priest convinced the king to have a temple built with many steps and a throne painted with scary pictures. Then he made idols to be worshipped along with the god-king.

"Grandfather. Why do unbelievers eat people?"

"Hmm. Some believers even eat people too! It is a sin called backbiting and we have to guard against it."

The people of Ad then went into the desert and conquered a people who lived in a beautiful green valley. The old king Ad died and his son Tanuh became king. Tanuh's son Shaddad became king after him and Shaddad's brother Abdullah had a son named Hood (a).

The people of the tribe busied themselves with making idols and other things out of gold they found in nearby caves. Hood (a) went to another cave to be away from the people, where he received his prophethood from the angel.

"Why did one man find gold and one man found the angel?" Sulayman asked.

"Hmm. Allah (s) knows what we are seeking. In your life, you need to decide what you are looking for. The treasures of this world, or the treasures of the next world."

Hood (a) became overseer of the slaves and cared for them and taught them about Allah (s).

Hood (a) with the people of Ad.

The people of Ad ordered Hood (a) to beat one of the slaves, but it gave that slave no pain and no marks appeared on his back, and with this miracle he invited the people of Ad to become believers and he told them about the gardens of paradise.

"Are the gardens of paradise like this garden?" asked Sulayman.

Grandfather smiled. "They are similar. There are rivers, fountains, trees and flowers, but the gardens of paradise are endless. This garden only goes about 5 minutes' walk that way."

"Too far, too far!" Yusuf chirped. Yusuf was tired from the walk and refused to go any farther.

When king Shaddad heard about this he ordered his people to make a beautiful garden on earth called the Gardens of Iram to prove that he was a god and could make the most beautiful garden. This garden was constructed in the Wadi Ahqaf over a period of 20 years.

While a tribe of idol worshippers from Mecca came to see this garden, King Shaddad boasted that as a god-king he could order the rain to come. Because of his arrogance the land became dry. King Shaddad sent some people from his tribe to Mecca to pray for rain and it happened that one of the party was a follower of Hood (a). This believer and the others who brought idols prayed for rain. Three clouds came and the follower of Hood (a) heard the clouds speak.

The first cloud was white and full of snakes and scorpions.
The second cloud was red and full of fire.
The third cloud was black and full of scorching wind.

The unbelievers thought that the black cloud was full of rain.

The black cloud that came to destroy the people of Ad.

This cloud approached the Wadi Ahqaf and the Angel Jibrail
(a) came to warn Hood (a). Hood (a) tried to warn the king but he
would not listen. Hood (a) gathered the believers and brought
them to a cave to hide from the black cloud.

The cave where Hood (a)
and his followers sought refuge in Jordan.

The scorching wind and avenging angels descended and killed the
unbelievers of Ad within a week.

> *"Was it that cloud?" Sulayman pointed at some*
> *threatening clouds approaching the garden. Just then a*
> *breeze picked up. Yusuf squeaked and hid under the park*
> *bench. Grandfather bent down and looked at Yusuf*
> *upside down. "Boo!" He tickled Yusuf and brought him*
> *up on his lap.*

Even when King Shaddad witnessed this destruction he did not
accept the one God.

After the storm ended Hood (a) took his followers to Mecca. Hood (a) is buried near the maqam of Ibrahim but the location of his maqam is not known for certain.

One of the companions of the Prophet Muhammad (s) named Abdullah saw the Gardens of Iram and we will all see these gardens on the Day of Resurrection.

Grandfather stood up, waved his stick at the cloud saying a quiet prayer, "Falammaa ra awhu 'aaridam mustaqbila awdiyatihim qaaloo haazaa 'aaridum mumtirunaa; bal huwa masta'jaltum bihee reehun feehaa 'azaabun aleem,"[1] *and led the boys up the path and out of the garden as rain began to fall on the far side of the garden avenue.*

"Come, this cloud will wait a little but not long."

"Did you talk to the cloud Grandfather?"

"You can talk to clouds if you speak their language."

---

[1] "Then, when they saw the (Penalty in the shape of) a cloud traversing the sky, coming to meet their valleys, they said, "This cloud will give us rain!" "Nay, it is the (Calamity) ye were asking to be hastened! - A wind wherein is a Grievous Penalty!" (Surah al Ahqaf [46] ayat 24)

Yusuf stopped took the stick from Grandfather and turned around, waved it at the cloud and shouted for it to go away. The cloud floated closer and Yusuf screamed and ran ahead of them on the path home.

When the boys had gone inside for lunch Grandfather went to the back orchard with his orange seed. He said a prayer quietly "Taraz zaalimeena mushfiqeena mimmaa kasaboo wa huwa waaqi'um bihim; wallazeena aamanoo wa 'amilus saalihaati fee rawdaatil jannaati lahum maa yashaaa'oona 'inda Rabbihim; zaalika huwal fadlul kabeer,"[2] and lifted his stick. A beautiful garden slowly became visible behind the olive trees with fountains and flowers and trees of all sorts.

---

[2] "Thou wilt see the Wrong-doers in fear on account of what they have earned, and (the burden of) that must (necessarily) fall on them. But those who believe and work righteous deeds will be in the luxuriant meads of the Gardens: they shall have, before their Lord, all that they wish for. That will indeed be the magnificent Bounty (of Allah.)" (Surah ash-Shurah [42] ayat 22)

If you looked closer you would see that the fruits glittered like jewels and the tiles in the fountains were made of lapis and malachite. He took the seed from his pocket and made a hole with his stick in the soft earth of one bare spot in the avenue of fruit trees. He planted the seed, watered it from the fountain and gathered some lemons from the tree next to him. As he turned to go back to the orchard the orange seed sprouted up out of the earth and began climbing towards the sun. He brought the lemons to the house for their lunch and told the boys there would be ripe oranges for their lunch tomorrow.

The interior of the maqam of Hood (a).

The maqam of Prophet Hood (a) in the Hadramawt of Yemen and Allah (s) knows best.

6 SALIH (a)

"No Sulayman, we are not buying a camel," Grandfather shook his head. He was taking the boys to see the carved cliffs of Petra in Jordan and there were many camels all over the valley floor. Sulayman was on his tenth ride around the site.

They tried to put Yusuf on a small foal camel but he was having none of it. He was scared of camels. He did not want to go up on the big camel with Sulayman either.

"But my camel can live on the terrace and take me to school!" wailed Sulayman.

Yusuf squealed and hung onto Grandfather when the little camel stood up. He patted Yusuf on the head and gave him a candy from his pocket.

It was getting late and they had to leave the valley before dark, so Grandfather asked the nice old Bedouin man to let Sulayman ride the camel out of the valley, where they were invited to stay with the man and his family near at their camp. When they got back to their tents the boys were bundled up by the campfire playing with sticks while the Bedouin family brought tea. Grandfather took out his prayer beads and the boys played with sticks in the fire while Grandfather began his story of the people who lived in the Valley of Hijr.

Some descendants of the people of Ad migrated to the Valley of Hijr two hundred years after Prophet Hood (a). These people followed a king named Thamood and they took the Valley of Hijr and killed the people there and the caravans that passed as well. Prophet Salih (a) was born to one of the chieftains of Thamood and was soon orphaned. He was not like his people because he wanted to work among the slaves instead of only enjoying the fruits of their labor. Salih (a) saw the slaves of Thamood as the children of Adam (a) and not as lesser beings.

The people of Thamood did not want to live in mud brick houses any longer because rains and earthquakes were damaging their houses. They made their slaves dig homes for them out of the mountainside.

"Did they use hammers?" asked Sulayman. "Can I use a hammer and make a building in the rock? I promise I won't hurt myself." Sulayman waved the stick he lit on fire a little too close to his brother and Grandfather looked doubtful.

15. The Rock

The auntie of Prophet Salih (a) tried to corrupt him with wine and Salih (a) fled into the wilderness where he found the Angel Jibrail (a). The Angel announced the prophethood of Salih (a) and called him to guide his people. The slaves and the low born followed Salih (a) and he asked them to be patient with the unbelievers. When the believers among the Thamood followed the teaching of Salih (a) they began to see greater fruit from their work.

Salih (a) built a mosque out of the mountain and called the believers there to pray. After that they were to declare their belief publicly and hide it from the unbelievers no longer. Salih (a) addressed the unbelievers himself when a man named Salif tried to stop him. Salif demanded a miracle from Salih (a) even though this would bring destruction on the unbelievers who would not listen to reason or understand the responsibility that comes with a miracle from Allah (s).

The people asked that the boulder become a camel and that camel would have a foal. Salih (a) asked for the miracle and the boulder spilt and a camel emerged. After some time, the she camel had a foal and Salih (a) admonished the people to leave the camels in peace.

Salih (a) making dua for the miracle of the she camel.

"If I ask for a miracle can I have a camel?" asked Sulayman.

Yusuf shook his head. "No no no camel!" he squeaked.

The camel was thirsty so Salih (a) brought her to the well, and when she drank all the water the people feared there would be no more. But miraculously the well filled again with water. The camel gave milk to all who approached her with good intention on every other day.

"Is camel milk good or yucky?" asked Sulayman. The Bedouin man brought the boys some little cups with camel milk.

"Good!" Yusuf squeaked after he sipped his cup. Sulayman looked doubtful so Yusuf drank the second cup.

One day Salif, the enemy of Salih (a), killed the she camel because the idol worshipers had told him it was the only way to bring back the girl he loved. The unbelievers that followed Salif tried to find and kill the followers of Salih (a), but they could not find them and were killed by falling rocks and boulders thrown by angels.

Salih (a) sought the camel foal once he heard that the she camel was slaughtered and saw the foal disappear into the split boulder. Now that the camels were gone Salih (a) told the people that they had three days before Allah's (s) punishment would fall upon them. The first day they would turn red, the second saffron yellow and the third day they would turn black. The fourth day they would be destroyed. After delivering this prophecy he took his followers to the mosque on the mountain.

> "You're turning yellow!" Sulayman pointed to Yusuf.
> Yusuf screamed and started crying when he looked down
> at his hands in the fire light. Grandfather frowned at
> Sulayman and put Yusuf on his lap to let him play with his
> prayer beads.

The unbelievers turned red and yellow and then black just as Salih (a) said and on the fourth day some say an earthquake destroyed them, and some say a rain of fire, but Allah (s) knows best. For seven days, the believers heard the screams and destruction and when it had finished Salih (a) led the believers out of that place.

This is thought to be the place on the Arabian Peninsula that Salih (a) brought the believers after they left the Valley of Hijr.

The boys had fallen asleep near the dying fire and Grandfather covered them over with some warm woolen blankets. The she camel and her foal were sleeping as well and Grandfather spoke to the old Bedouin man looking after them in whispers. They rose and the old Bedouin led Grandfather away. Some among the Bedouin thought that there was a treasure in the caverns at Petra, but the wise knew that treasure was not gold. The old man took Grandfather around to a secret path to the old mosque on the mountain above the valley. As they entered the mosque carved out of the cliff face they found a vast cavern and cave system behind the prayer space. There were cisterns and aqueducts lifting and pouring water in ingenious ways, enough water to fill the whole valley below. The old man went to a place in the prayer niche and moved a rock there. He took out some bundled papers and handed them to Grandfather, who unwrapped them carefully on the carved stone table. It looked like Arabic but it was older. The papers had complicated drawings of all the water works and instructions on how to build and maintain a water rich city in the middle of a desert, ancient but advanced technology that could even collect water from wind and air. They made wudu in the spring for Isha and stayed to pray Tahajud and Fajr. When the sun began to light the edge of the sky they returned to the tents where they found the fire smoldering and a large stone boulder behind the fire with the boys still sleeping next to it. The old Bedouin man laughed and patted the *boulder before they both lay down to sleep.*

Salih (a) led his people to Mecca and is possibly buried there and Allah (s) knows best.

The maqam where people honour
the Prophet Salih (a).

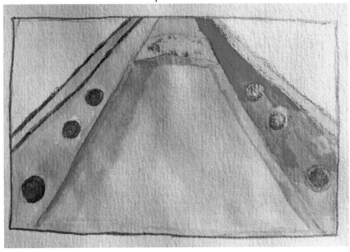

7 IBRAHIM (a)

Sulayman and Yusuf were playing in the garden when a song bird landed on the rosebush near them and started singing. Yusuf pointed to the bird and smiled. Sulayman shook the rosebush with a stick but the bird held fast. As he shook the bush harder the bird jumped onto his head and pulled out some of his hair.

Sulayman ran from the garden screaming that a bird was killing him and bumped right into Grandfather. When he asked what was wrong Yusuf ran up.

"Bird!" squeaked Yusuf.

Grandfather looked where Yusuf pointed and saw a nightingale hopping from rose to rose. It stopped briefly and sang in their direction.

Grandfather nodded at the nightingale and patted Sulayman on the head.

"The nightingale loves the roses very much Sulayman, and you should not disturb him," Grandfather advised. Yusuf started giggling as Sulayman waved his arms around complaining about the bird.

"Bee!" squealed Yusuf.

He pointed to a bee crawling on one of the roses in front of them. The bee took off and flew in Sulayman's direction, floating around his head. Sulayman started screaming and ran into the house.

"Come Yusuf, I will tell you the story of the Nightingale and the Bee, if we can find where your brother is hiding. Your brother should not harass the animals of Sayyidina Ibrahim. I fear he is going to learn the hard way."

Sulayman screamed from inside the house and the bee flew out and back toward the garden.

"Bee!" Yusuf pointed.

Sulayman was shouting that the bee had stung him. Grandfather looked at his arm and said he was not stung and explained that bees die when they sting and the bee was in the garden alive and well.

He took a jar out of the cupboard and gave them each a spoon of honey.

"Bees are blessed animals because of what they did for Ibrahim (a), and now I will tell you his story."

After Prophet Salih's (a) time the believers followed the rivers and settled near the Tigris and Euphrates.

For a time, their belief was strong but after some time they failed
to heed their Prophets. King Nimrod thought he was a god like
Pharaoh and consulted soothsayers about his dreams. One night
he dreamed that a great star, larger than the sun, fell on his head,
and so he asked them what this meant. Most of the soothsayers
said something flattering to Nimrod. But one young man told him
that dream had another meaning. He said that the lady Nimrod
had recently wed would have a son that would be greater than
Nimrod.

Nimrod would have no one greater than he so he killed his bride with a sword and her head fell into the fountain. Now the other soothsayers told the king that another woman who was expecting a baby in the land would have a son to challenge Nimrod and bring a new religion to destroy the idols. Nimrod ordered all the women pregnant with a child to prison and any male child born to them to be killed.

> "Why did he want to kill a baby? A baby can't do anything," Sulayman frowned.

> "Hmm. Babies grow up Sulayman. And once they do they can do all sorts of things."

The mother of Ibrahim (a) was older and so did not know she was with child, till one day she went to the temple and the idols screamed and scared her away because her child would be their destroyer. She ran to tell her husband Azar who was a maker of idols, and he told her to keep quiet or Nimrod would find out and kill her and the child.

When the time for the birth came Azar told her to go to the temple to give birth, but the idols screamed so loud that she ran into the wilderness and there met the Angel Jibrail (a). The angel opened a cave in the mountain where she found water and all she needed for the birth. After the baby was born she wrapped him and rested. The cave had been dressed like a pavilion in paradise and servants cared for her and the baby. The baby remained in the cave for his protection, and she returned to her home in the day and spent the night in the cave with the baby Ibrahim (a).

The cave was far from the Euphrates river in Damascus but the Angel brought her quickly so it seemed not long. This cave is still visited by pilgrims in Damascus. Some say that the story of Ibrahim (a) and Nimrod occurred in a place called Urfa in Turkey where there is the Cave of Urfa and a pond that holds the water that put out the fire of Nimrod.

One day his mother found the cave surrounded by wild lions, wolves and leopards. She feared they had eaten the baby but she found him protected by the angels. The baby was sucking on his fingers and from each finger there flowed nourishment. There was butter, honey, rose water, syrup and milk. Each day the baby grew as much as one month and matured quickly. Eventually Ibrahim (a) asked if he and his mother were alone in the world and so she brought his father Azar.

Yusuf took his thumb out of his mouth and looked at it carefully. He frowned.

"Honey!" He showed his thumb to Grandfather. "Tell it to give honey for Yusuf."

Grandfather chuckled.

Ibrahim (a) remained in the cave for 10 years for his protection from Nimrod who was still killing mothers and babies. One day he asked his mother to show him the world outside the cave. When they were outside the cave Ibrahim (a) said "There is no power and no might except with Allah (s), the Sublime, the Almighty."

When the star rose Ibrahim (a) asked his mother what it was and she said it was God. The moon came up and he thought this was God because it was greater. When the sun came he thought this one was God but in the end they all diminished with time and Ibrahim (a) understood that these things were not God. His mother was concerned that Ibrahim (a) did not believe as they had and she worried that he was the one child Nimrod sought.

When Ibrahim's (a) parents came to take him back to the city of Nineveh on the banks of the Euphrates river he told them he had been instructed by the Angel that there was only one God and that their religion of many gods and idols was incorrect. His parents were frightened and confused but told him he must obey them and return to Nineveh. Ibrahim (a) was a good son and so he obeyed his parents.

Azar desired that Ibrahim should carve idols and sell them in the market like they did but instead Ibrahim abused the idols and told them if they were truly gods they could protect themselves. The people thought he was crazy and would not buy from him. One man asked why he did not respect the idols. Ibrahim said he did because the idols cooked food and baked bread. The man said no the idols do not do these things because they are only wood and cannot work. Then Ibrahim told the man that if these idols were only wood then he should worship the one true God and say there is no God but God. The man did and he felt happy and light and so in this way Ibrahim (a) began to instruct the people of Nineveh.

His father was upset when he found out and beat Ibrahim (a), but his mother said it was not his fault that he did not know their religion because he had been raised in a cave. She told Azar to send their son to the sorcerers in the temple of idols to learn their religion. Azar apologized to the people for Ibrahim's (a) behavior and then told Ibrahim he was sorry for not teaching him well and took him to the temple. Ibrahim (a) made dhikr there and prayed in the direction of the Kaaba, but no one knew.

One day when the people were at a feast Ibrahim (a) said he was ill and stayed at the temple. After they had gone he destroyed all the idols except the largest. He left the axe in the hands of that idol. When they returned and asked him what had happened he said that the large idol had destroyed the others, but they said an idol cannot destroy other idols. When they questioned Ibrahim (a) he asked them why they worship idols that cannot defend themselves.

"Can I make an idol Grandfather? And then I can smash it!" Sulayman asked eagerly.

"You are smashing everything already," said Grandfather.

"But I want to smash an idol! Where can I get one? What do they look like?"

Grandfather pointed to Yusuf's teddy bear.

"They are looking a bit like that."

Yusuf started crying and tried to hide his teddy under the blanket as Sulayman pounced to grab it. There was screaming and wrestling until Sulayman emerged from the blanket with the teddy and started pounding the little bear into the floor. Yusuf was crying and trying to stop Sulayman. Grandfather put Yusuf on his lap and told Sulayman to give him the bear. Grandfather gave the bear back to Yusuf and dried his nose with a tissue.

"Mr. Bear is not an idol Sulayman. Yusuf does not pray to Mr. Bear."

"No touch it my bear!" Yusuf screamed.

It was at this time that Ibrahim (a) received his prophethood and he was brought before Nimrod by the people. Ibrahim (a) asked Nimrod what he wanted without bowing or waiting for the king to speak first. Nimrod asked him why he did not bow and Ibrahim (a) said that he only bows to Allah (s). Nimrod asked who Allah (s) was and Ibrahim (a) said that Allah (s) is the one true God and the giver and taker of life. Nimrod had a man brought before him and had him beheaded and then brought another man and set him free. Nimrod then said he is also the giver and taker of life.

Ibrahim (a) said that Allah (s) makes the sun to rise in the east and set in the west and invited Nimrod to make the sun rise in the west. Angered by that Nimrod ordered Ibrahim (a) to be imprisoned with no water for a year on the mountain in a very hot place.

In this time, even the father of Ibrahim (a) would not accept the one true God, and then Nimrod and many of his people decided to get rid of Ibrahim (a) for good. Nimrod wanted to burn Ibrahim (a) and told all the people to bring one log for the great bonfire.

The horses and donkeys would not carry the wood but the mules did, and so they were cursed and cannot have babies to this day for helping Nimrod. For a year they collected wood, and once the fire was lit Shaitan inspired them to use a catapult to throw Ibrahim (a) into the fire. The angels tried to save and protect Ibrahim (a) from the fire but he declined.

"Why did Ibrahim want to go into the fire?" asked Sulayman.

"He did not want to go but he was submitting and putting himself in Allah's (s) hand," answered Grandfather.

"Why did Allah (s) want Ibrahim (a) to go into the fire?"

"Hmm. Allah's (s) Prophets have very hard tests and their example teaches us how to have trust in Allah (s). Without this example, we cannot understand how to be servants to our Lord. By allowing Ibrahim (a) to go into the fire Allah (s) is trying to show us something."

When Ibrahim was launched into the fire the logs became green trees again, a spring of water came and Ibrahim sat in a beautiful garden in the middle of the fire. The bee brought water to put out the fire and this is why the bee now gives honey which is healing for mankind. The nightingale threw itself into the fire for the love of Ibrahim (a) and the Lord showed the nightingale that Ibrahim (a) sat unharmed in the fire and put the nightingale on a rosebush. The nightingale then asked to know the names of Allah (s) and these names became the beautiful song of the nightingale. Many other animals brought water to put out the fire except the lizard who fanned the flames and this is why the lizard is cursed.

Just then they heard a nightingale trilling in the courtyard.

"Bird!" Yusuf said.

Sulayman hid under his blanket. He mumbled that the nightingale should be cursed for pecking him in the head.

The daughter of Nimrod saw that Ibrahim (a) was safe in the fire and told her father. Nimrod was flown by eagles to see this himself. When he found Ibrahim (a) unharmed he asked how he was saved from the fire and Ibrahim (a) said that the one true God had saved him and Nimrod asked if he could be accepted by the one true God as well. Ibrahim (a) told him yes but some say that Nimrod had killed his daughter for accepting the one true God and his people then feared him even more. Ibrahim (a) was released because they could not kill him.

Nimrod had a very high tower built and said he would kill Ibrahim's (a) One God from the top of it. He tried to kill the One God with a bow and arrow he shot towards the sky, and an angel brought a fish to be pierced by the arrow so that Nimrod would believe he had succeeded. When Nimrod showed the arrow to his people they believed he had killed the one God, except Lot (a) the nephew of Ibrahim (a), who did not believe it.

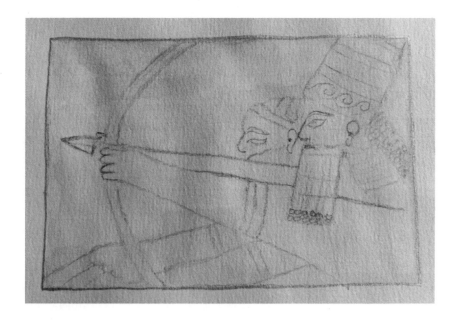

The fish asked why it was killed and the Lord ordered that the fish should not be slaughtered by the knife, but by suffocation. The blood of the fish fell to the ground and white poplar trees grew from the drops.

Prophet Ibrahim (a) married the daughter of his uncle. Her name was Sarah (r) and she was a believer. Ibrahim (a) then brought Sarah (r) and his nephew Lot (a) with him and migrated out of Nineveh. When they reached Palestine Lot (a) remained there to teach the prophecy received by Ibrahim (a).

Ibrahim (a) and Sarah (r) continued to Egypt with a caravan but before they reached the gates Ibrahim (a) hid Sarah (r) in a box. He was afraid that if they saw how beautiful Sarah (r) was that they would give her to the Pharaoh.

"Could she breathe in the box?" asked Sulayman.

"Yes."

"How big was the box?" Sulayman held his arms wide.

"It was big enough to fit a lady inside, bigger than you, smaller than me."

When they discovered her, they asked Ibrahim (a) who this beautiful woman was and he told them she was his sister so that they would not kill him and it is true that they were brother and sister in their faith. Sarah (r) was very brave. When they brought her to the Pharaoh she resisted him saying she was the wife of a Prophet and he should not touch her. When the Pharaoh tried to touch her his hand shriveled and he asked her to pray for him to be healed. He tried to touch her 7 times before he gave up and apologized to her for his bad manners. The Pharaoh then gave her a slave named Hajar (r) who was the grandchild of the prophet Salih (a).

After a time, they returned to Nineveh to appeal to Nimrod once more to accept the One God. Nimrod asked where the army of the One God was and Ibrahim (a) said that the army was comprised of mosquitos. These mosquitos came out of the poplar trees that had grown from the blood of the fish that Nimrod had shot with the arrow. Nimrod prepared his army, but he himself hid in a room secured with a keyhole that spiraled 7 times because in truth he was afraid to face the army of Allah (s). The mosquitos that emerged from the poplar trees were not ordinary mosquitos and they ate through the armor of the soldiers and drank their blood and devoured them all, even their bones.

One mosquito who was lame traveled through the spiral lock into the room where Nimrod hid himself. The mosquito battled Nimrod for 3 days before flying in through his nose and into his head. It began to eat his brain and this was very painful so Nimrod would order a servant to hit his head to stop the mosquito for a moment. One day a slave hit his head with a large rock and split his head in two. The mosquito flew away having grown to the size of a small bird.

A mosquito flew by Sulayman's ear and he screamed and waved his arms around. The mosquito landed on the wall near the ceiling and looked down at them. Sulayman threw things at it and it just flew around until he stopped and then landed again. Finally, Sulayman hid under his blanket so the mosquito couldn't find him.

Ibrahim (a) left Nineveh once more and bought some land to start a farm, but the people were afraid of him now and would not sell him the things he needed to farm the land. Returning from the market one day he filled his bags with sand so that the people would not know he had returned with nothing. But Allah (s) had filled his bags with wheat and grain. He was surprised to smell the baking bread. Sarah (r) brought him some and said she found the flour in his bags.

Ibrahim (a) and Sarah (r) had no children and Sarah (r) suggested that Ibrahim (a) should marry Hajar (r) so that their family might have children. Ibrahim (a) and Hajar (r) were married and had a son named Ismail (a). Sarah (r) was not able to bear having Hajar (r) live near her anymore, so Ibrahim (a) took them into the desert and the angel Jibrail (a) told him to leave them where the camel sat down. The place the camel sat was very hot and dry with no plants or water. After Hajar (r) ran out of food and water she went to search for some provision. She ran between the hills of Safa and Marwa 7 times in search of water. Then she saw the foot of Ismail (a) strike the ground. From the spot where his foot struck water gushed out of the ground forming the well we call Zam-Zam. A voice from the well told her that the water was sufficient for food, drink and illness and she thanked the Lord for this special water.

"Why didn't Ibrahim come back and bring her more food."

"Ibrahim (a) knew that Allah Almighty would provide for Hajar (r) and Ismail (a)."

Sometime later a lost caravan found this place with Hajar (r), her son Ismail (a) and the well of Zam-Zam. The people of the caravan had an illness that was instantly cured by the water and so they asked Hajar (r) if they could return with their families and build a city in this place. In that way, the city of Mecca was founded.

Ibrahim (a) then had a dream where the Lord ordered him to sacrifice his son Ismail (a). He had this dream 70 times and the dreams of Prophets are true. Hajar (r) prepared Ismail to go out with his father but after they left Shaitan came to her to say that Ibrahim (a) was going to kill her son. She recognized Shaitan and drove him away saying that if the Lord took her son that she would accept this. Shaitan then approached Ibrahim (a) and Ismail (a) trying to deceive them, but he failed. Ismail (a) threw three stones at Shaitan injuring him in the valley of Mina.

"I want to throw stones at Shaitan."

"Hmm," said Grandfather. "When you go on Hajj[1] you will."

"But I want to throw stones at Shaitan now. I don't want to wait till I'm old!"

"Well I am going soon. If you have memorized your second juz[2] I will take you."

"But a juz is so long!" wailed Sulayman.

Yusuf started crying. Grandfather rubbed his head.

---

[1] Pilgrimage to Mecca

[2] Section of Quran

"Juz too long." Yusuf squeaked.

"You have many months. And If Yusuf has one juz and Sulayman has two then I will take you."

"Too long!" Yusuf buried his face in his blanket.

"You will be ready before your brother Yusuf because you have 1/2 a juz already and Sulayman only has one and he has to learn a whole other juz."

Ibrahim (a) tried to cut Ismail (a) 70 times, but the knife would not cut and Ismail (a) remained whole and unwounded. Both father and son sincerely tried to submit to the will of God. When the knife did not cut Ibrahim (a) asked "why" in a special state of consciousness and used a speech called "Hal," and the knife said "Why did the fire not burn you?" The knife responded that as the fire was ordered not to burn the knife was ordered not to cut.

Ibrahim (a) and Ismail (a)

The angel Jibrail (a) appeared and brought the ram given by Habil (r) (in the story of Adam [a]) and it was sacrificed in place of Ismail (a). Jibrail (a) then said to name 3 prayers and Allah (s) would accept them. Ibrahim (a) prayed for Allah (s) to have mercy on the Nation of Muhammad (s). Ibrahim (a) prayed that the Nation of Muhammad (s) should not suffer. Ibrahim (a) prayed that Allah (s) forgive the Nation of Muhammad (s). He knew about the Nation of Muhammad (s) from his education in the cave.

Ibrahim (a) and his son Ismail (a) then had a discussion about who had made the greater sacrifice that day, and in the end Allah (s) said that Ibrahim (a) had done so because if he would have killed Ismail (a) he would feel that burn in his heart for the rest of his days while Ismail (a) would enjoy paradise.

One reason given for this trial of Ibrahim (a) is that he had slaughtered a cow calf before its mother one day when he had no other food for his guests. Another reason is that once Ibrahim (a) prayed against a group of wicked people and they died so Allah (s) wanted Ibrahim (a) to experience the pain of sacrificing his precious son to make him understand that the creation of Allah (s) was precious as well.

When Ibrahim (a) was 100 years old and Sarah (r) was 80 years they were visited by four guests who would not eat the food Ibrahim (a) gave them. The guests revealed that they were angels sent to bring the news that Sarah (r) was going to have a baby boy named Ishaq. The unbelievers thought it was funny that a couple so old had a baby. Ishaq (a) and Ibrahim (a) looked so similar that people could not tell them apart, and so Allah (s) made the beard of Ibrahim (a) white.

Ibrahim (a) and Ismail (a) rebuilt the Kaaba in the place where the angel Jibrail (a) touched his wing to the ground. A cloud came to wash the ground and the black stone was returned to the Kaaba from Mount Abu Qubays. Ibrahim (a) taught the people the rights of Hajj where we go around the Kaaba, running between Safa and Marwa where Hajar (r) had run, standing on Mount Arafat where Adam (a) and Eve (r) were reunited, and throwing stones at the pillars in Mina against Shaitan.

Ibrahim (a) and the Kaaba

The next year Ibrahim (a) returned with Sarah (r) and Ishaq (a) to perform Hajj and they prayed for the Nation of Muhammad (s) together.

"I don't want to wait to go on Hajj," Sulayman wailed.

"Most people are waiting their whole lives," said Grandfather. "People used to walk for months and years to reach Mecca for Hajj."

"I can walk!" said Sulayman.

"Too far!" Yusuf wailed. "Yusuf no walk."

The angels asked their Lord if they could test Ibrahim (a) to see whether he had Allah (s) in his heart or dunya. Ibrahim (a) received 4 guests who would not eat, and one of them recited the prayer "Praise to the all Holy, our Lord of the angels and the spirit." Ibrahim (a) found this prayer so beautiful that he gave all he owned to hear it again. Because the angels could not take the wealth of Ibrahim (a) with them Allah (s) said that these gifts were under His Own care.

One day a fire worshiper came as a guest to Ibrahim (a). They disputed and Ibrahim (a) gave his guest food but did not like to eat with him. After the fire worshipper left Allah (s) reprimanded Ibrahim (a) for not receiving his guest with sincere hospitality. Ibrahim (a) went in search of the man for 10 days and then carried him back on his shoulders. The fire worshipper was so impressed with the efforts of Ibrahim (a) that he became a believer.

"How did Ibrahim (a) carry the fire worshipper?" asked Sulayman.

"Allah (s) gave him great strength," Grandfather answered.

"Too heavy," Yusuf shook his head.

After this Ibrahim (a) met a series of ascetics. One could make water appear where he struck his foot. Another would fast for months at a time waiting for a guest. Another lived in a cave making dhikr who would break his fast only once every 2 months. Then he sought another man in a cave that was a beautifully decorated mosque. This ascetic said he would break his fast once every 3 months, and their *iftar* appeared on a floating tray. Ibrahim (a) was tested by a scary tiger that would have eaten him if he were not sincere.

Then the ascetic took him to an island where he lived and confessed that he had prayed for many years that he could meet Ibrahim (a) and now that he did he passed away and was buried by Ibrahim (a). Then the angel came to take Ibrahim (a) to the Gate of Repentance which he said would be open until the sun rose in the West. When Ibrahim (a) was trying to guide Nimrod, he asked him if he could make the sun rise from the West and Nimrod could not, but Allah (s) can and will.

On the day, the angel Azrail (a) visited Ibrahim (a) and announced that Ibrahim (a) had been named the friend of God. Ibrahim (a) wanted to know how living things were brought back to life. Azrail (a) demonstrated with some birds where the four winds collected the pieces of a dead bird and brought them back and the bird came alive once more.

Sometime after a very old man visited Ibrahim (a). He was weak and unable to feed himself. Ibrahim was near in age to this old man and so he asked his Lord to take him before he became an invalid.

The old man turned into the Angel Azrail (a) and took the soul of Ibrahim (a) gently. He was buried near his wife Sarah (r) in Khalil (Hebron) in the Holy Land.

Grandfather looked down. Yusuf was sleeping and Sulayman was snoring under the blanket where he had hidden from the mosquito. Grandfather uncovered Sulayman a little and the mosquito slowly descended. When Grandfather whispered something to the mosquito it hovered for a moment before it turned to fly away. He went to take wudu (ablution) and the Nightingale trilled in the garden as the adhan for Isha prayer echoed through the courtyard.

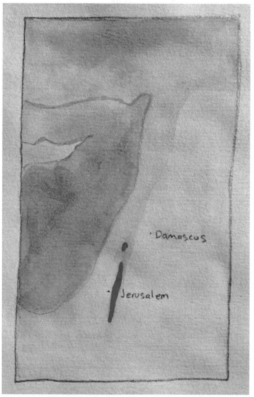

Map of the Holy Land

The Maqam of Ibrahim (a) in the Holy Land.

8 ISMAIL (a)

Grandfather handed Yusuf a little cup of water while Sulayman filled his little flask. They sat for awhile resting after their long journey to Mecca. Yusuf looked into his empty cup and said "Zam Zam bye bye."

Sulayman's flask was overflowing and he splashed water all over his ihram. "Uh oh!" He said. The man who greeted them at the well closed Sulayman's flask and mopped him up, laughing.

"Never mind," said Grandfather. "You will be dry in a few minutes."

"When Hajar (r) and Ismail (a) came to this place with Ibrahim (a) there were no trees. There was no water. There was no food. No houses. No people. Nothing." Grandfather waved his tasbih beads to show them that the whole area around them had been barren.

"What were they doing here?" asked Sulayman.

"Here is hot," said Yusuf.

"Ibrahim (a) brought Hajar (r) here with their baby on the order of his Lord. Their story is a very important one. The things that they were starting here are the things that we will do again to remember how their Lord has honored them and us."

Ismail (a) was the son of Prophet Ibrahim (a) and Hajar (r). By his Lord's order Ibrahim left Hajar (r) in the desert with the baby Ismail (a). Soon after Ibrahim (a) departed their water and food ran out and baby Ismail (a) started to wail. Hajar (r) began to look for water for her baby.

She ran as fast as she could between Safa and Marwa searching for water 7 times and Ismail (a) began to turn blue in the face from screaming. His little foot hit the sand and water began to come forth from that place. Hajar (r) scooped out the sand around this place to contain the water and the well of Zam Zam was formed. The Awliah say that if she had not formed a pool but had let it run it would have become a river.

> Grandfather was walking between Safa and Marwa while holding Yusuf's hand. The other pilgrims were running and Sulayman was far ahead of them. Sulayman reached the end and came running back down and nearly knocked over the Hajis in his path. Yusuf clung to Grandfather as Sulayman sped past them. Sulayman had listened maybe a little too closely to Grandfather's story of Hajar's run between Safa and Marwa.

Hajar (r) and Ismail (a) stayed in that place and when caravans came by she gave them water. They found the water to be healing and soon people began to settle there.

After some time, Ibrahim (a) had a dream that he must sacrifice the thing that he loved the most. He began by sacrificing his animals but this was not the thing he loved most. After he saw this dream 70 times he took his rope and his knife and returned to Mecca. Ibrahim (a) told Hajar (r) to dress Ismail (a) and prepare him to go out. Shaitan approached Hajar (r) and Ismail (a) three times, trying to tell them that they should not obey Ibrahim (a) because he meant to harm Ismail (a).

"Why did Ibrahim need a rope and a knife?" asked Sulayman.

"He took the rope and the knife to sacrifice Ismail (a)."

"But why didn't Ismail run away."

"Because Ismail (a) and Hajar (r) trusted their Lord and Ibrahim (a). When Allah (s) told Ibrahim (a) to leave Hajar (r) and Ismail (a) in the desert they all obeyed and Allah (s) took care of them. They did not listen to Shaitan then and they did not listen to Shaitan now."

Sulayman and Yusuf walked on with Grandfather and they saw people picking up pebbles.

"Why are they taking the rocks?" Sulayman tugged on Grandfather's hand.

Yusuf stopped and started picking up stones.

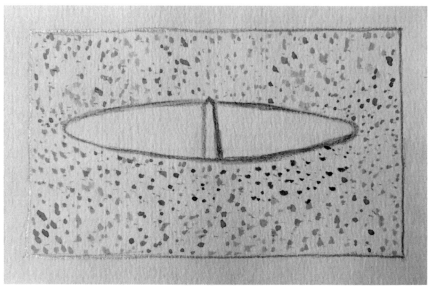

The Jamarat

When Shaitan approached Ismail (a) with the news his father would kill him Ismail (a) threw stones at Shaitan to drive him away. This is why we collect and throw pebbles on the Hajj.

Ismail (a) consented to be sacrificed by Ibrahim (a) on the order of Allah (s).

He told Ibrahim (a) to tie him and turn his face away so that it would be easier to make the sacrifice. Ibrahim (a) tried to cut Ismail (a) 70 times but he was protected by the Angel, and the sheep sacrificed by Habil (son of Adam (a)) was used instead.

Sulayman threw his stones hard at the pillar just as Grandfather did and Yusuf's pebbles fell short because he couldn't throw very hard. Grandfather gave him more pebbles and he kept trying.

Ismail (a) lived in Mecca with his mother most of his life and married one lady whom Ibrahim (a) disapproved of because she was not hospitable. When Ibrahim (a) came to visit she would not receive him. After divorcing the first lady Ismail (a) married Sayyida (r). She was blessed by Ibrahim (a) and her children were to become part of the line of Prophets which made her very happy. The Prophet Muhammad (s) came from the family of Ismail (a).

When their Hajj was nearly completed the boys went with their Grandfather to find a sheep. They found a shepherd on their walk and the boys played with the sheep and petted their heads and soft wool while Grandfather spoke with the old Bedouin shepherd.

The shepherd showed Grandfather all the sheep that were mature for the sacrifice but Grandfather kept looking around the field. He came to a small group of bushes and parted the branches with his staff. There was a large sheep grazing behind the bush and Grandfather told the shepherd that he wanted this one. The shepherd looked reluctant. He said this sheep was special. This sheep was the father of the whole herd and had been with the shepherd a very long time. Grandfather asked him how long, but the shepherd was very old and said he could not remember. Sulayman took the staff from the shepherd and started pushing the sheep along and chasing the stragglers. Yusuf petted the big sheep and told him not to worry.

The shepherd and Grandfather could not come to an agreement but the shepherd invited them to dinner. They met the shepherd's family and son. The shepherd told Grandfather that his son and daughter in law had no baby even though they had been married for 10 years. Grandfather smiled and asked if they wanted to have a baby. They said yes so Grandfather said that if the shepherd helped him sacrifice the old sheep that he'd asked for he would make dua that the couple would have a baby. The shepherd immediately agreed and kissed Grandfather's hand.

Grandfather went with the shepherd to get the sheep with the boys straggling after. Together with the shepherd they separated the old ram from the herd and took him far away from the other animals. Sulayman and Yusuf sat on a rock and watched as Grandfather laid the animal down with the head turned towards qibla and petted the animal gently till it was still. He spoke to the sheep softly and said "Bissmillah - Allah hu Akbar."

He cut the sheep quickly with a sharp knife and the shepherd helped him hang the animal to drain the blood. They returned to the shepherd's tent and Grandfather made a long dua for the shepherd's family before they sat down to eat dinner together. Sulayman and Yusuf were very quiet after the sacrifice. Yusuf looked sad and Sulayman was distracted.

"Grandfather, was the sheep scared?" Sulayman asked on their walk back after dinner.

"Sheep get blood," said Yusuf.

"The sheep needs to be calm, so it will not be scared."

"Did it hurt the sheep?"

"Sheep is hurt!" squeaked Yusuf.

"Yes, but we use a very sharp knife so it will hurt less."

"Why did you cut the sheep?"

"We cut the sheep to remember how hard it was for Ibrahim (a) to try to sacrifice Ismail (a)."

"Was it hard for you to cut the sheep."

"Yes. This was a special sheep."

"The shepherd didn't want to give him?"

"No, he did not want, but he did."

"Why was that sheep special?"

"That sheep was a descendant from the sheep of Habil, that replaced Ismail (a), and it is not the same as other sheep."

"Why did Allah want Ibrahim to cut Ismail?"

"Allah (s) wants us to love our Lord more than anything else. More than our family even."

"Why was it hard for you to cut the sheep?" asked Sulayman.

Grandfather turned to Sulayman as tears came from his eyes and he patted him on the head. "Because Sulayman I love you and Yusuf very much. I am ashamed because I do not think I could do what Ibrahim (a) did."

Sulayman looked up at Grandfather and started crying too. Grandfather gave him a hug and Yusuf cried.

"Sheep hurt," Yusuf whimpered.

This is thought to be the place where Ibrahim (a) sacrificed the sheep.

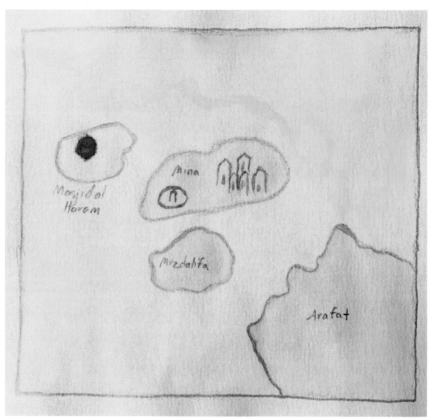

Hajj Journey

"I am not a good boy like Ismail (a). I would have run away,"
Sulayman cried. Grandfather started laughing and crying
at the same time.

"We are weak servants Sulayman. But we will try harder.
We will see what is your goodness."

~

The next day Grandfather walked slowly around the Kaaba with the boys on their final tawaf.

"Kaaba is too big!" Yusuf squeaked. "Too long for Yusuf walk!" Grandfather took Yusuf's hand and led him along.

"Where did the Kaaba come from?"

"There is a Kaaba in the heavens, there was a Kaaba here built by Adam (a) and this Kaaba was built by Ibrahim (a) and his family."

The Bayt ul Mamur

The Kaaba constructed by the family of Ibrahim (a).

As they passed the black stone Sulayman asked why people were kissing it.

"That is the Hajar al-Aswad. It is an original stone from the first Kaaba. It was hidden in Mt. Qubays when the flood came. It was white but it turned black from all our sins."

"Mama can clean it. She makes all my shirts clean again."

"This is not the kind of dirtiness we clean with soap. We clean with wudu, prayers, dhikr and our Hajj. These things will clean us."

"But we can't clean the stone?" asked Sulayman.

Grandfather laughed. "First we clean ourselves and then we will see."

"Can I kiss the stone?" Grandfather nodded and when they came around again Sulayman kissed the stone and Grandfather lifted Yusuf to do the same.

"Yusuf hot!"

Grandfather raised his hands and made a quiet dua. "Allazee ja'ala lakumul arda firaashanw wassamaaa'a binaaa 'anw wa anzala minassamaaa'i maaa'an fa akhraja bihee minas samaraati rizqal lakum falaa taj'aloo lillaahi andaadanw wa antum ta'lamoon."[1]

---

[1] "Who has made the earth your couch, and the heavens your canopy; and sent down rain from the heavens; and brought forth therewith fruits for your sustenance; then set not up rivals unto Allah when ye know (the truth)." (Surat ul-Baqra 22)

Little wispy clouds started forming over their heads and rain started to fall. The water began to climb around their ankles until Yusuf was up to his waist. Grandfather handed his staff and tasbih (prayer beads) to Sulayman and picked up Yusuf as they finished their final tawaf and swam for the exit.

The flooded Kaaba

"Will the stone be clean now Grandfather?" asked Sulayman.

~

Later Sulayman showed Grandfather a little black rock he found on the ground while they were in the cave with Grandfather the day before. Grandfather took it from Sulayman and closed his hand.

"Is it part of the black stone, that was in the mountain, the mountain with the cave?" asked Sulayman.

Grandfather smiled but did not reply. After a few moments of gripping the rock tightly he blew on his hand and opened his fingers. There was a little glittering gem in his palm.

"You made the black stone white!" said Sulayman with huge wide eyes. Grandfather smiled and held his finger to his lips.

Sulayman took the gem and looked at it in the light. "It's all glittery and rainbows."

"Put it in a safe place," said Grandfather. Sulayman put the gem in his satchel and closed it carefully.

"One day, when you are old enough to marry you will find a good lady like Sayyida (r). You will give her this gem in a ring and you will be a good husband to her and father to her children."

"How will I know who she is?" asked Sulayman.

Grandfather smiled. "The same way I knew your Grandmother was the one."

After he buried his father later in life Ismail (a) returned to Mecca with his wife Sayyida (r). The children of Ismail (a) became the Bedouin people who live in the desert. Ismail (a) became a prophet and was sent to guide the people living near Mecca. He led them for 60 years and was very successful. He is buried near his mother Hajar (r) in Mecca.

Awliah on the Hajj

Painting of the Maqam of Hajar (r)

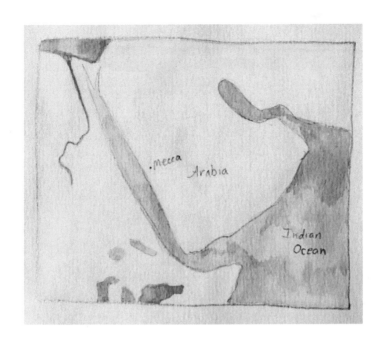

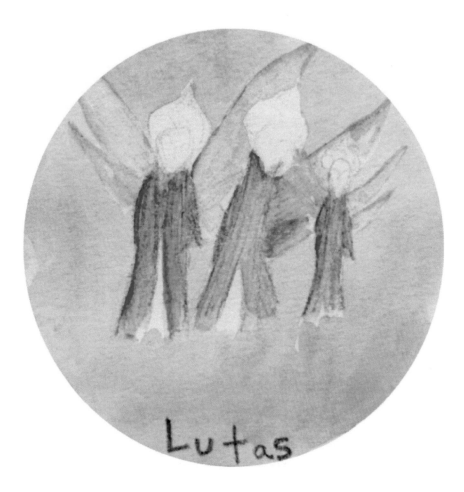

Lutas

9 LUT (a)

Sulayman and Yusuf were playing near the house in the garden when two cats on the roof began to have a terrible noisy fight. Pieces of ceramic tile fell to the ground onto their heads together with the screeching cat. They boys ran away screaming and covering their heads while the cat ran the other way.

Grandfather came out of the zowiah (prayer room) to see what the commotion was all about. They boys told him that the sky was falling and the stones were hitting them on the head. Grandfather took a small piece of tile from Yusuf's hair and examined it carefully before laughing.

"Come to have your supper and then I will tell you the story of Prophet Lut (a) and a time when the sky was really falling."

The boys followed after him with their hands still up over their heads.

Lut (a) was a prophet in the time of Ibrahim (a) and they were both sent to guide people. Lut (a) was the nephew of Ibrahim (a), and when the Angel Jibrail (a) announced his prophethood he went to the Dead Sea region to guide the people living there.

"Why is it called the Dead Sea?" asked Sulayman.

"They are calling it the Dead Sea because it is too salty for the little creatures to live in it."

"Where is the Dead Sea? Is it in Hell?" asked Sulayman.

Grandfather took his atlas off the shelf and showed the boys a drawing of the Dead Sea.

Lut (a) married one lady from among these people. She did not become a believer but she bore him four daughters who were believers.

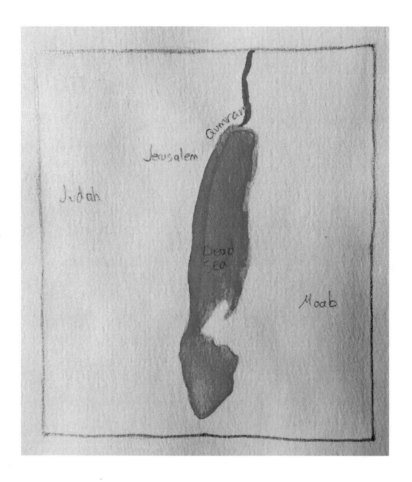

The people that Lut (a) was trying to guide were very wicked, and when three angels came to visit Lut(a) in the shape of three young men he worried that the people of that place would kidnap them.

"How can you kidnap an angel?" asked Sulayman.

"You cannot, Lut (a) was trying to protect his guests and he did not yet know they were angels." Grandfather took his tasbih from his pocket and began his awrad (silent recitation).

When a mob of badly intended people came Lut (a) offered his daughters in marriage to them and said to please leave his guests in peace. When the mob broke down the door to the house of Lut (a) the angels revealed themselves and Azrail (a) blew upon the people so that they were blinded. The angels then warned Lut (a) that destruction was coming and he should gather the believers and leave this place.

Angels

They were warned not to look back at the rain of burning clay that destroyed the people in a black cloud.

"Is that the same black cloud as came in Prophet Hood's story?" asked Sulayman.

"Maybe." Grandfather tilted his head to one side.

Each falling piece of clay had the name of the person that it would kill written upon it. Not obeying the divine command the wife of Lut (a) did look back and perished as well when one of the stones of Hell fell onto her. The cities that were destroyed were turned upside down by the wing of Jibrail (a) and the place became the Sea of Lut (a) or the Dead Sea.

The fallen cities in the story of Lut

Lut (a) then joined Ibrahim (a) in Jerusalem and later traveled to Mecca where he passed away and was buried somewhere near the Kaaba.

This is a maqam for the Prophet Lut (a)

Grandfather looked down and saw that the boys were snoring softly. He took a small flask of salty water from his pocket and a small jar of black mud from his other pocket and placed it inside the toy chest after saying a special prayer, "Keela mea makkannee feehi raabee haayrun fa aeenoonee bi kuvvatin ac'aal baynakum va baynahumm radman."[1] He patted the boys gently and turned out the light before going to take wudu for Isha prayer.

---

[1] "That in which my Lord has strengthened me is better. Only my Lord will help me with that Force. I will make a shield force between you and them." (Al Kaf 95)

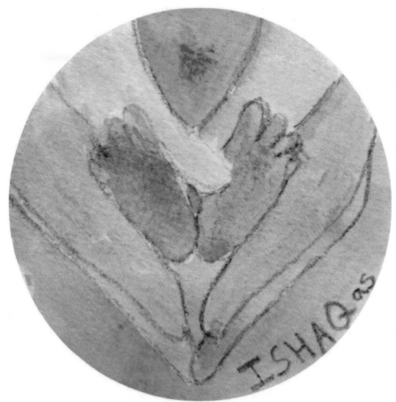

Ishaq (a) the Miraculous Baby

10 ISHAQ (a)

Sulayman wanted his mother to give him an apple from the tree near the clothesline in the back garden. After pestering her for several minutes he gave up and went off to look for something to stand on so he could reach himself. Mother finished hanging their little shirts and trousers and reached up into the tree for an apple. Just then Yusuf ran up and she handed the apple to him, forgetting which child had been wanting one.

Yusuf was bewildered but took the apple and wandered off with it. Moments later Sulayman returned with a step stool and saw Yusuf with the apple. He screamed and threw the stool before setting off to chase Yusuf. Yusuf dropped the apple and ran back to his mother, trying to hide behind her. She sorted out their squabble and gave them each another apple and reminded Sulayman to be gentle with his little brother. But the apple Yusuf had dropped remained discarded on the ground at the edge of the garden.

A few days later Grandfather found Sulayman poking the apple with a stick and squealing about all the worms crawling around inside it. Sulayman wanted to know how all the yucky worms got into the apple. Grandfather sat down under the tree and said to bring Yusuf and he would tell them the story of a quarrel between brothers that caused a fitna so large it took many many years to mend.

"When we are angry this makes a hole in our hearts like the hole in this apple. The hole allows bad things to come inside our hearts and lets the badness grow until the heart is like this apple, rotten and crawling with worms."
Sulayman looked shy and Yusuf looked nervous.

The miraculous baby sent to Ibrahim (a) and Sarah (r) was now a man. Ishaq (a) was a Prophet in the lands that extended from Jerusalem to the Dead Sea and northwards to Sham.

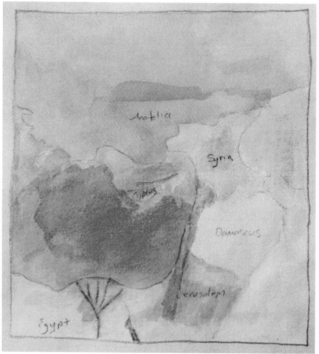

The Near East

When Ishaq(a) began to look for a bride he went to a well and asked the ladies there for water. Only one lady offered him water and he discovered that she believed in the unity of God and was not an idol worshiper.

After the Prophet Ismail (a) passed away Prophet Ishaq (a) lead as a Prophet for 100 years. As he aged he became blind and when a famine came to his land he did not know until he noticed how thin his little grandson had become. Only then he found out that the people had no food.

"How did he know the little boy became thin if he was blind?" asked Sulayman.

"Hmm," Grandfather stopped. "Well if you close your eyes can you still hear?"

Sulayman closed his eyes. "Yes."

Grandfather drew Yusuf close to Sulayman and put his arm in Sulayman's hand.

"And this boy. Is he big or small?"

"Small."

"Fat or thin?"

"Thin. He must be starving for sure." Sulayman opened his eyes to see Yusuf looking down at his arms and tummy in bewilderment.

"I not starving. Yusuf eat porridge!" he squeaked.
Grandfather chuckled.

Ishaq (a) prayed for guidance and was told to move his people to
the land of Jarrar. The followers of Ishaq (a) prospered there
but were eventually driven out by the unbelievers of Jarrar. They
continued to move until they found the Well of Resting after
wandering for 30 years.

*"Why didn't they stop and ask for directions? Why didn't
they have a map?"* asked Sulayman.

"Hmm," said Grandfather. *"They may have asked for
directions but the place they were looking for was not on a
map."*

"Why wasn't the well on a map?"

*"Maps are for the time they are drawn. The earth changes
but the map does not."*

"Why?" squeaked Yusuf.

"A map is like a picture. Do you draw pictures?" The
boys nodded.

"Is your picture looking like the thing you are drawing?"
The boys looked at each other and then shook their heads no.

"In this time people were not using maps so much. It is different now."

Ishaq (a) had two sons As and Yaqub (a). When they were in the womb of their mother As wished to be born first and fought with Yaqub (a). As was large and strong with a hairy body while Yaqub (a) was a gentle shepherd.

Maqam of Ishaq (a).

When the time came for Ishaq (a) to bless one of these two sons to succeed him he preferred As, but their mother Rifqa (r) preferred Yaqub (a). She told Yaqub (a) to slaughter a sheep and come to his father wearing the furry sheep skin so that his father would think it was As and give his blessing instead to Yaqub (a). After Yaqub (a) received Ishaq's (a) blessing Rifqa (r) told Yaqub (a) to run away so that As would not kill him for their deception.

"How is As going to kill Yaqub," Sulayman asked.

"As is not going to kill Yaqub (a)."

"But how was he going to try? A sword? A bow and arrow?"

"Hmm," Grandfather paused a moment. "As was very strong but he was not a warrior. A rock maybe, like Qabil. But Yaqub (a) was protected by Allah (s)."

"Oh," said Sulayman, clearly hoping for something more dramatic. Grandfather patted Yusuf on the head as he scooted under his arm.

As went in search of Yaqub (a) who was hiding in a cave and he did not find him. Yaqub (a) traveled to Madian to look for his uncles as his mother told him and this journey called Isra is the reason why the descendants of Yaqub (a) are called the Children of Israil.

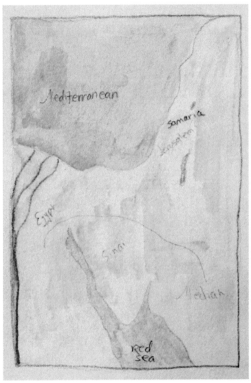

Yaqub (a) fell in love with the younger daughter of his uncle and asked to marry her. His uncle agreed to the marriage as long as Yaqub (a) agreed to look after his uncle's sheep for 7 years. When the time for the marriage came Yaqub (a) was given the elder sister Leah (r) not the younger sister Rahil (r) and so he worked for his uncle another 7 years until he was allowed to marry Rahil (r) as well. Among the 11 sons of Yaqub (a) was Yusuf (a), the son of Rahil (r).

Rahil's (r) family were idol worshipers and she took one idol with her when she left Madian with Yaqub (a) and was cursed by her father. When she gave birth to Beniamin[1] soon after she passed away.

"What did the idol look like?"

"Hmm," Grandfather frowned. "Idols like this were small. Little statues. Have you ever seen a statue, like you are finding in a museum?"

Sulayman nodded but looked doubtful. Grandfather stood up and went over to the bookshelf. He picked up a very large and heavy book with a coarse tan binding.

---

[1] Beniamin means the son of my sorrow or to burn inwardly in Syriac.

He sat and opened the book and turned the thick colored pages covered with large photographs, maps and drawings. Finally, he stopped and pointed to a funny little man with a beard and kohl rimmed eyes. The boys started pushing to see closer.

"They were looking something like this."

"And why did they have these? Why did they have a statue?"

"They thought that the statue is a god and they thought that there is more than one god."

"But why did they think that?"

"They thought that because their parents believed it."

"But why did their parents believe that Allah (s) could be in a statue?"

"Hmm," chuckled Grandfather. "You are asking the right question. In those times, there were jinn that would come and sit inside the statue. The jinn would speak and make some things happen that the people could not explain. In those days people were often confused by the power of the angels and the jinn and thought that these things with invisible powers were gods."

Sulayman looked at the statue and after a long while looked up at Grandfather. "Is that why the Prophets are scared when the angel comes to speak to them – because they didn't know what an angel is?"

Grandfather nodded. "Something like this. Or they were not sure if the one speaking to them was being an angel or being a jinn."

"But angels don't go in statues?"

"No. Angels do not go in statues."

"So, Allah (s) does not like us to listen to jinn in statues?"

"Yes. They are tricky ones."

"But Allah (s) made them too?"

"Yes."

"Why?"

"Allah (s) made mosquitos also. Many things that we may not like, but mosquitos like us, no?" Grandfather laughed and Sulayman frowned.

Yaqub (a) then returned to the lands of his father and when they encountered As the sons of Yusuf (a) said they were the sons of the Lord's servant who had run away and returned to make peace with his master. As was still angry with Yaqub (a) but then mercy entered his heart. As embraced and forgave Yaqub (a) and shared the lands of their father with him.

"How did the mercy get into his heart? Did it get in through the same hole as the worm in Yusuf's apple?"

Yusuf stared down at his chest and looked worried.

"Yusuf no want hole. Worm is yucky!" he squeaked.

"Hmm," Grandfather paused and took out his tasbih beads. "We are believing that Allah (s) cannot be contained in a statue. But we are believing that Allah (s) can be contained in one thing. Do you know what that one thing is?"

Yusuf looked down at his chest again and Sulayman frowned.

Grandfather pointed at the center of Yusuf's chest. "Allah (s) can be contained inside your heart. So, mercy can come from inside your own heart if you listen."

"Yusuf have Allah (s)! Yusuf no have worm!" He pointed to his little chest and ran off to tell his mother. "Mama Mama! Yusuf have Allah!"

Grandfather chuckled and Sulayman put his head inside his shirt to get a better look at his chest.

"Tomorrow I will tell you more about Yaqub (a), but now it is time for tea." Sulayman followed Grandfather back to the house as the call to Asr prayer sounded and the sun sank lower.

This is the maqam where people come to honour Sarah (r) the mother of Ishaq (a).

YAQUB(as)

11 YAQUB (a)

There was a large splash and much screaming and wailing in the garden. Mother came running and found Yusuf sitting on a rock at the bottom of the garden well. She called for help and Grandfather brought a ladder.

He stepped slowly down into the well where Yusuf was now hysterical because he saw a snake. The snake slithered away quickly and Grandfather carried Yusuf up out of the well.

It was some time before they found Sulayman hiding in the back garden up in a tree and questioned him about how Yusuf came to be at the bottom of the well. Yusuf was washed, dried and set up on a couch with warm blankets and some hot cocoa in a beautiful golden cup with funny little pictures on it. He was quite happy now but Sulayman was sullen. He wanted cocoa as well and his mother said no because he was to be punished for pushing Yusuf down the well.

The large metal basin where mother had bathed Yusuf still sat on the floor and Sulayman was looking into it as Grandfather peered over his shoulder. Sulayman looked at Grandfather in the reflection and Grandfather began to tell them the tale of Yaqub (a) and his sons.

One day Yusuf (a) looked upon his reflection in the mirror and thought what would his worth be if he were sold as a slave. He did not know that one day his Lord would answer his question.

Yaqub (a) lived with his family in the land of Canaan. The 10 brothers of Yusuf (a) were shepherds and grew jealous when Yaqub (a) kept Yusuf (a) near him all the time so that he could gaze at the beauty of Yusuf (a).

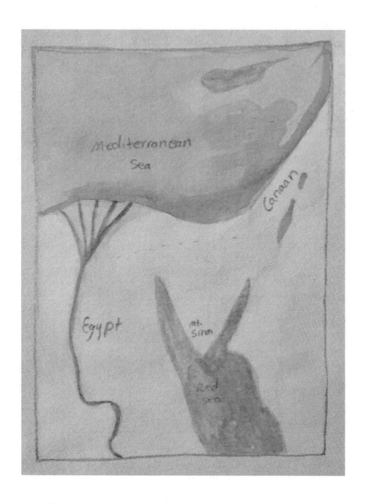

When Yusuf (a) was 12 years old he told his father that he had seen 11 stars and the sun and moon bow before him. Yaqub (a) advised Yusuf (a) not to tell this to his brothers because of their jealousy. He then foretold that Yusuf (a) would learn from his Lord the interpretation of dreams as the other prophets of his house had been given.

"Why did Yaqub tell Yusuf not to tell anyone about his dream?"

"Hmm. Some people cannot accept that they are not the most beloved. But there is a high price to being loved as much as Yaqub (a) loved Yusuf (a). Sometimes it is better to hide our love when there are others who are hurt by witnessing that love. Yaqub (a) loved all his sons, even the ones who were jealous of Yusuf (a). So, we must learn from Yaqub (a) and be kind to all our family and people around us, not make it harder for them by saying we love this one better or that one more."

Sulayman frowned. "Everyone loves Yusuf more than me. They give him bussies and hugs. They give him candies and presents."

Grandfather rubbed Sulayman's head. "People like to look at sweet faces. They may not notice the strong and quiet ones whom Allah (s) gave greater gifts. A good memory, a powerful voice, a strong heart, these are gifts as well Sulayman."

Sulayman put his head on Grandfather's knee. He was quiet for a moment and finally said, "I need hugs and bussies too Grandfather." Grandfather hugged Sulayman's shoulders and smiled.

"And so, it will be for the rest of your life. There are always people who get more attention and presents. But you can have something even better than that."

Sulayman looked up, "Have what?"

"The love of Allah (s) and the rewards of Paradise are much greater than anything we are finding here on earth. You can be having thousands of hugs and candies. More than you can ever count."

"How do you get to Paradise?" Sulayman asked, now intrigued.

Grandfather smiled. "Well that is not easy. But you have the strength to get there Sulayman because Allah (s) gave you much strength. But you need to use that strength to love and protect your brother. Allah (s) made you his guardian. Can you watch over him and protect him from harm?" Sulayman nodded.

"Then you have taken your first step to Paradise." Sulayman smiled and asked how many kinds of candy he would find there and what it looked like.

The brothers of Yusuf (a) learned about the dream from their sister and Shaitan inspired them to bring their brother out to play and kill him. They promised to look after Yusuf (a) well but their father Yaqub (a) was afraid. When he finally allowed them to take to Yusuf (a) out to play they were rough with him and then threw him into a well.

Painting of Yaqub (a) and his sons.

Yehuda convinced the brothers to leave Yusuf (a) in the well rather than to kill him. The angel Jibrail (a) caught Yusuf (a) as he fell and set him gently on a rock with a big snake. Jibrail (a) told the snake to be quiet but it could not hear because the snake was deaf.

"No like snake!!" Yusuf wailed.

"Why was the snake deaf?" asked Sulayman.

Grandfather chuckled. "Are you ever seeing a snake with ears?"

"Why was there a snake in the well?"

"Hmm. This snake was there to speak against Yusuf (a)." Grandfather took his tasbih (prayer beads) from his pocket.

"Why?" asked Sulayman.

"Some snakes are sent to test us. To see if we will be afraid or keep strong faith. They wind around us and squeeze until we cannot breathe but we have to remain unmoved in our hearts," Grandfather began turning the beads in his fingers.

"We have to not be scared?" asked Sulayman.

"Yes Sulayman," Grandfather nodded.

"Yusuf no like snake!" Yusuf squeaked.

The brothers returned to their father with a false story about a wolf that had eaten Yusuf (a) and showed him a bloody shirt to prove it. Yaqub (a) knew this was a lie because the bloody shirt was not torn at all but covered with the blood of a crow.

"Why didn't Yaqub make them bring Yusuf back?"

"Yaqub (a) was under the order of Allah (s) to be patient."

"Why didn't he go to the well and take Yusuf out himself?"

"Yusuf (a) had his own path and both father and son had to accept the will of Allah Almighty. Yaqub (a) did not know where the well was. He was old and blind. But more than that he knew that this was something he had to accept and that Allah (s) would reunite him with Yusuf (a) one day."

"Was it hard for Yaqub to do what Allah said?" asked Sulayman.

"It was the hardest thing in his whole life. There is nothing worse for a father than losing his child. It is so for all mamas and babas."

"Why are you crying Grandfather?"

"It is very hard thing to wait when you have lost a child."

Sulayman hugged Grandfather. "I won't go away. I promise."

"Inshallah."

A caravan soon passed the well and drew out Yusuf (a) upon a bucket of water. The leader of the caravan had dreamed that he would become more wealthy than the Pharaoh of Egypt when the moon fell from the sky and into the well.

While traveling with the caravan they passed the grave of Yusuf's (a) mother Rahil (r) and when he tried to go there to grieve the other slaves beat him because of their jealousy. A storm came raining hail upon the caravan and the leader knew that the punishment from above had a reason and so went in search for the cause. The leader wanted to kill the abusers of Yusuf (a), but Yusuf (a) said no, that he had forgiven them.

"Why did Yusuf forgive the people?"

"Hmm. It is not an easy thing to be a slave. Yusuf (a) had strong faith and he had pity for those that had none. The Prophets of Allah Almighty are sent to earth to help us have faith. If you were a slave, hungry, beaten, tired your whole life and now your master wanted to kill you for your mistake, how would you feel?"

"Bad," whispered Sulayman.

"Yes. Yusuf (a) saw how bad they felt in their hearts and he had great pity for them. He did not want to punish them. He wanted to help them and give them hope."

"How did he give them hope?"

"He gave them the one thing no one ever gave them before."

"What did he give them?"

"Mercy."

Yaqub (a) had a dream where Yusuf (a) sat upon a hill top surrounded by 11 wolves. 10 wolves tried to attack him and the earth swallowed Yusuf (a). When the brothers returned they brought to Yaqub (a) the blood stained shirt to prove that a wolf had killed him. Yaqub (a) asked his sons to bring him this wolf and the wolf spoke to Yaqub (a) saying that he had not eaten for 3 days while he searched for his milk brother. Yaqub (a) reprimanded his sons.

"How did Yaqub talk to a wolf?"

"Allah (s) gave him the ability to understand the wolf."

"Can I learn to speak wolf?" asked Sulayman.

"And what would you say to a wolf?"

"Do NOT eat me."

Grandfather started laughing so hard he cried.

Yaqub (a) was later reunited with his beloved Yusuf (a) in the land of Egypt over the affair of a stolen gold cup. This is the story of Yusuf (a) that we will hear another day. Yaqub (a) later died and was buried near to Ibrahim (a).

Grandfather looked down and saw that Sulayman had fallen asleep on his knee and Yusuf had dropped his empty cup on the ground. Grandfather tucked a blanket around Sulayman and picked up the cup and cleaned it carefully over the basin of water. He opened the large carved chest in the corner and took out a cloth, wrapping the cup and its delicate hieroglyphics from ancient Egypt. He placed the cup inside the chest near several small sharp fruit knives wrapped in tarnished linen and said a special prayer "Keela mea makkannee feehi raabee haayrun fa aeenoonee bi kuvvatin ac'aal baynakum va baynahumm radman,"[1] and closed the chest once more.

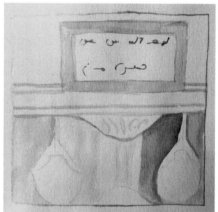

This is the tomb of Yaqub's (a) wife.

---

[1] "That in which my Lord has strengthened me is better. Only my Lord will help me with that Force. I will make a shield force between you and them." (Al Kaf 95)

This is a cave where the family of Prophet Ibrahim (a), Ismail (a) and Yaqub (a) are buried.

The maqam of Yaqub (a) in Jerusalem.

YUSUF(as)

12 YUSUF (a)

Yusuf grabbed Sulayman's neck and kissed him on the cheek and would not let go. Sulayman screamed and kicked and dragged Yusuf down the hall and thought it was a great game. He said Yusuf was making him wet with spit and snot and frantically tried to get away.

*Yusuf chased him through the house trying to kiss him
again until they crashed into the kitchen and knocked a
bowl of apples and mandarins all over the floor. They were
reprimanded and spent the next half hour collecting and
washing all the fruit and placing it back in the bowl under
the raised eyebrow of their mother.*

*When all was set right again they went out into the
garden to play and found Grandfather under an old
gnarled olive tree. They sat down with him in the shade.
He gave them each a small gummy candy wrapped in foil
and began to tell them the story of Yusuf (a).*

Yusuf (a) had the likeness of his mother Rahil (r) and both had 9
parts of the 10 parts of beauty sent to the world. The beauty of
the Prophet Muhammad (s) is not counted among the 10 parts
because his beauty is not of the earth and Allah (s) knows best.

In the land of Egypt there was a lady named Zulaykha (r)
who dreamed of Yusuf (a) before he came there. Lady Zulaykha
(r) was the most beautiful lady of her time. When she dreamed of
Yusuf (a) he said that he was the king. When she woke she told
her father and so he offered her hand to the king. When
Zulaykha (r) saw the king, she realized that this was not the same
person she saw in her dream and she was sad because now she
was married to the wrong king.

The king saw the boy Yusuf (a) at the market after he had arrived with the caravan in Egypt. He wanted to bring the boy to live with him as a son to himself and Zulaykha (r) who had no children. Yusuf (a) was set on a scale and all the gold in the treasury was not enough to match his value, but the man who found Yusuf (a) in the well accepted the gold.

"Was Yusuf fat?"

"What?" said Grandfather.

"Was Yusuf fat? Is that why he was so heavy?" asked Sulayman.

Grandfather laughed. "Yusuf (a) had a heavy worth not a heavy body."

"Yusuf no fat," Yusuf pointed to his belly.

"Our Yusuf needs to eat more food," Grandfather said.

When Yusuf (a) had grown up Zulaykha (r) took Yusuf (a) into a room sealed with 7 doors and 7 locks. There she tried to kiss him and he resisted because there he saw Ibrahim (a), his father Yaqub (a) and Angel Jibrail (a) in the room with him, warning him not to make a mistake.

The Lady Zulaykha (r) and Yusuf (a)

He turned to run away through the door that Angel Jibrail (a) opened, and Zulaykha (r) tore his shirt when she tried to stop him. The king saw the torn shirt when Yusuf (a) came out of the room and knew that Zulaykha (r) had torn it.

"Why did she tear his shirt?" asked Sulayman.

"She did not want Yusuf (a) to leave her," explained Grandfather.

"Why?"

"She loved him for many many years and she could not stop herself."

"But why didn't she want him to leave?"

"Hmm. Have you ever wanted a candy when your mother told you no?"

Sulayman nodded slowly. Yusuf hid the candy wrapper behind his back.

"Did you go and try to get candy where no one could see?"

Sulayman nodded and Yusuf shook his head.

Grandfather raised his eyebrow.

"Well for Lady Zulaykha (r) Yusuf (a) was like the best bonbon ever made and she could not restrain herself."

"Was Yusuf (a) made of chocolate or gummy bears?" asked Sulayman.

"I want gummy bear!" squeaked Yusuf with his mouth full of candy.

The other ladies of the city came to know about this incident and Zulaykha (r) was shamed, so she invited them to come and eat at the palace and when she served them fruit she gave each a little knife. When Yusuf (a) came into the room they all cut their own hands in astonishment.

"Why did they cut their hands?" asked Sulayman.

"Hmm. They were looking at Yusuf (a) and not at the fruit and knife in their hands and then they cut themselves," explained Grandfather.

"Did they have to go to the hospital?" asked Sulayman.

"No shots!" squeaked Yusuf, who ran to hide behind the bush.

Sulayman showed Grandfather his hand. "I got cut here, but I was not looking at Yusuf. I was cutting and I slipped. The doctor had to sew me with a needle," said Sulayman seriously.

"No needle!" Yusuf wailed from behind a bush.

"Yusuf fell and cut his lip once. They had to sew his lip."

"No sew me!" Yusuf screamed now in hysterics and making the bush shake.

Yusuf (a) was then put in prison after he would not kiss Zulaykha (r) and his prison became like a paradise while she slipped into madness. She would give money to anyone who brought her news of Yusuf (a). In this way, she gave away all her wealth and became poor, wandering in the wilderness.

Two prisoners came to Yusuf (a) to ask the meaning of their dreams. Yusuf (a) told them their fate, for one would serve the king and one would be punished for trying to poison the king. All this came to pass and Yusuf (a) asked the prisoner who was a cup bearer to tell the king of his innocence. The cup bearer forgot to ask and Allah (s) was not pleased that Yusuf (a) asked the aid of the cup bearer but did not ask the aid of Allah (s). Yusuf (a) prayed for forgiveness and it was granted.

While Yusuf (a) was in prison a new king came to power and had a dream of 7 fat cows and 7 lean cows, 7 green ears of corn and 7 withered. The cup bearer who had been in prison with Yusuf (a) went to him with the dream of the king. Yusuf (a) said that there would be 7 years of plenty and 7 years of famine. The king called for Yusuf (a) and freed him, making him the master over the storehouses so that they would store food for 7 years in preparation for the 7 years of famine.

"I had a dream that I lost my tooth," Sulayman pointed to his teeth.

Yusuf reached over and tried to open Sulayman's mouth wide and look at his teeth.

"It was just a dream," he mumbled over Yusuf's hands.

"Have you been doing your prayers?" asked Grandfather.

"Well, I forget sometimes."

"This dream can mean that you are missing prayers."

*Yusuf got down on the floor and made sajda. "No teeth,"
he said, examining the carpet.*

When the famine came the people sold everything to buy food
and by the 7th year they sold themselves into slavery to have food.
The famine spread to the land of Canaan where Yaqub (a) and
the 11 brothers of Yusuf (a) still lived.

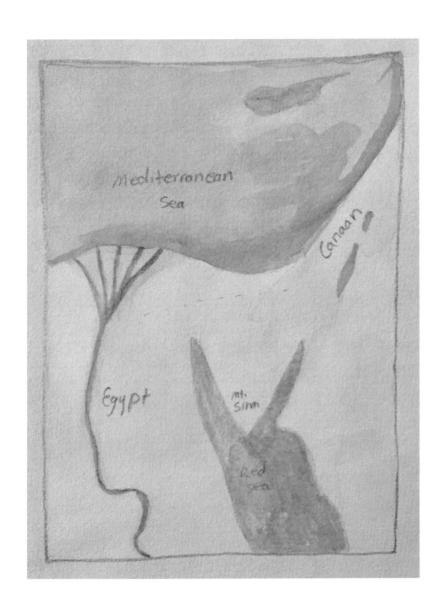

His brothers came to Egypt to find food and Yusuf (a) recognized them. He asked after the 11th brother and told them to bring him to Egypt. When the brothers brought Beniamin to Egypt. Yusuf (a) hid a gold cup in Beniamin's bag. Just when the brothers were about to leave a messenger came and stopped them, searching the bag of Beniamin for the stolen cup. Beniamin became the prisoner of Yusuf (a) and the brothers had to return to Yaqub (a) without their brother.

"Why did Beniamin steal the cup? Did it have cocoa?" asked Sulayman.

"No, he did not steal the cup, Yusuf (a) placed the cup there secretly so that the messenger would find the cup in Beniamin's (a) bag," explained Grandfather.

"Why did Yusuf put the cup in Beniamin's bag?"

"He wanted to keep his brother with him in Egypt."

"Why?"

"He had a plan."

When the brothers returned for more grain Yusuf (a) sent his shirt, that had been the shirt of Ibrahim (a) with his brothers to his father Yaqub (a). While Yusuf (a) was lost Yaqub (a) had grieved so much that he became blind. When his sons brought him the shirt of Yusuf (a) Yaqub (a) laid it over his eyes and he could see again. Yusuf (a) and Yaqub (a) were reunited and all the people of Egypt and all the angles wept. Yusuf (a) freed all the slaves in thankfulness.

After some time Yaqub (a) returned to Jerusalem and had a vision of a beautiful company of people. He asked to join them and the Angel Azrail (a) told him first to drink from a cup that was the draught of death. Yaqub (a) was buried near to Ibrahim (a).

"Was that the same cup that Beniamin stole?"

Grandfather smiled.

"I want cocoa! In Yusuf cup." squeaked Yusuf.

"I want cocoa too! It's not his cup, I found it in the toy box," Sulayman pointed to the carved toy chest in the corner of the room.

"Maybe after dinner, if your mother says you ate well," Grandfather said.

When Yusuf (a) became king, he gave a great feast on the order of his Lord and the angel told him that one person had not been served at the feast. This person was a lady that lived beneath an old gnarled olive tree. When he came to see this lady he did not recognize her as the Lady Zulaykha (r). She took from him a riding whip and blew upon it. She handed it back to Yusuf (a) and it burned his hand. She told him that this is the heat of her love for him and it burnt him like a hot coal. He asked how she could carry that burning love as a weak woman while he could not even touch it as a strong man.

Yusuf (a) prayed for Zulaykha (r) to return to youth and she was transformed. They were then married and prayed to have sons that would be prophets. The prayer was accepted and the great feast prepared for the new King Yusuf (a) became their wedding feast. When Lady Zulaykha (r) became a believer all her love for Yusuf (a) became love for Allah (s) and she only wished to pray to her Lord. Yusuf (a) tore her wedding gown when she would not come to kiss him and he remembered the day she tore his shirt. Yusuf (a) and Zulaykha (r) had 11 sons.

> "Why did he tear her dress?" asked Sulayman. "Her mother will be cross. Mama is cross when I tear my trousers climbing the tree."

> "Well Zulaykha (a) was very beautiful and now he thought she was a gummy bear," explained Grandfather.

> "I want gummy bear," Yusuf wailed.

"Was she angry that he ripped her dress?"

Grandfather smiled. "No, she was not angry."

"Why not?"

"Ladies like to be gummy bears to their husbands."

Sulayman scowled in thought. "When can I have a lady gummy bear?"

"Well being a husband and a baba is a big responsibility. You have to protect your wife and give her a house."

"But I don't have a house," despaired Sulayman.

Yusuf pulled on Grandfathers hand and pointed to their treehouse in another tree. "I want gummy bear for my house."

"When will I get a house?" asked Sulayman.

"First you will prepare to study at Al Chemya, and after you have learned all you can there you will go out into the world and make your fortune. Then you will build a house and find a good lady and have children. You will sit in your garden and tell them stories one day inshallah."

When Yusuf (a) passed away he was buried in a marble coffin and sunk into the Nile until an old woman showed Musa (a) where to find it before the believers left the land of Egypt many years after.

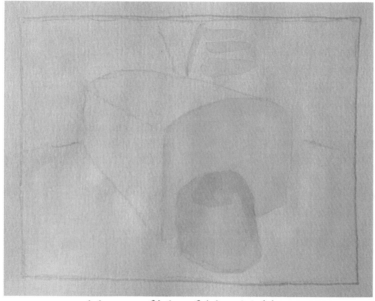

Maqam of Yusuf (a) in Nablus

Mother called them all to dinner and they followed Grandfather into the house, leaving the gnarled old olive tree behind. Tiny green shoots appeared at the end of each branch when Grandfather and the boys left as though the tree were becoming young again.

Please see our other books and projects at
https://muslimfamilytraditions.wordpress.com

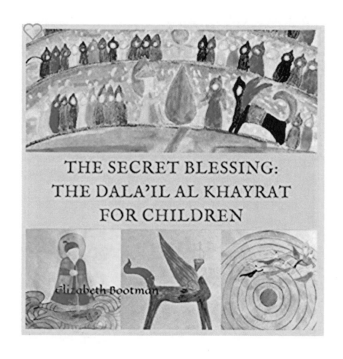

THE SECRET BLESSING:
THE DALA'IL AL KHAYRAT
FOR CHILDREN

Elizabeth Bootman

Made in United States
North Haven, CT
10 October 2022

25250730R00108